Ross Dawson's book brilliantly summarizes the precarious situation in which we humans find ourselves, as the data tsunami threatens to drown us. We need a plan to manage it—and its power—for human benefit. And that's exactly what this smart book offers, acknowledging but moving on from the usual litany of complaints and offering a practical model of transformational understanding far different from the forgettable how-to manuals that drive so much business publishing. This well-built volume is thoroughly wise, ever practical, and a remarkably timely guide as we peer ahead up the curve. I once ran a think tank in Washington with the strapline "Asking tomorrow's questions" because if you get the questions right, the answers flow. That's exactly what *Thriving on Overload* does. It may save your life.

—NIGEL CAMERON, President Emeritus of the
Center for Policy on Emerging Technologies

On the path to wisdom, purpose, and meaning, what can be more important than finding a way to hack your own cognitive stack? In his new book *Thriving on Overload*, Ross Dawson provides a comprehensive set of principles, mental models, and anecdotes to guide even the most voracious infovores on their journey to make sense of the world.

—MIKE WALSH, CEO of Tomorrow and
author of *The Algorithmic Leader*

A great refactoring is among us. Digital natives are competing with legacy analogs in almost every aspect of our lives. How we harness both the plethora and the power of information will determine the winners and losers in this dynamic economy. This must-read book shares the pragmatic secrets of how to overcome being overwhelmed and how to turn information into an unfair advantage.

—R "RAY" WANG, Founder, Chairman, and Principal
Analyst of Constellation Research and author of
Everybody Rules the World and *Disrupting Digital Business*

Reading *Thriving on Overload*, I didn't realize how many of these things I have been doing in my professional and personal life already, and also how many great apps and technology tools I wasn't using yet! Ross's book is an amazing compendium that can help even the most organized and fastidious person to improve their thinking and processes.

—JUSTIN BAIRD, Chief Technology Officer APAC at Microsoft

In a world where information can be debilitating, deceiving, or confusing, it's easy and even inevitable to miss what will help you learn, grow, and thrive. And sometimes it's not even about signal-to-noise ratios becoming overwhelming. It's signal-to-signal ratios where there is so much great content available. In this book, Ross will help you not only find the signal but also become part of it.

—**BRIAN SOLIS,** digital anthropologist, futurist, and *Wall Street Journal* bestselling author of *The End of Business as Usual*

Thriving on Overload is bursting with thoughtful strategies for optimizing your information intake.

—**LESLIE SHANNON,** Head of Ecosystem and Trend Scouting at Nokia

In a world where we measure content in zettabytes, finding the secret to navigating the right mix of skills, structure, and vision to thrive seems elusive at best, but not for Dawson. He gives us a road map not only for the present but for the future that is eminently achievable.

—**BRETT KING,** author of *Augmented* and *The Rise of Technosocialism*

We exist in a world in which many of us feel barraged with information. *Thriving on Overload* provides a thoughtful and invaluable structure that allows one to distill and make sense of this river of data. It is a great read.

—**STEPHEN POOR,** Chair Emeritus of Seyfarth & Shaw

Ross Dawson's *Thriving on Overload* will teach you how to maximize ROI on the scarcest resource in the universe: your attention.

—**ROBERT TERCEK,** Cofounder of The Futurists and author of *Vaporized*

Mind management is a core skill to manage stress and anxiety in an era where our mental health is increasingly at risk. This skill is essential not only for your own success but also for those whom you parent, coach, and lead. By reframing one's mindset and relationship with the information avalanche from overload to abundance and integrating the five superpowers laid out so clearly, one can transform obligation to choice, stress to joy, floundering to skilled, and ultimately drowning to thriving.

—**ANNALIE KILLIAN,** VP of Strategic Partnerships at sparks & honey

All of us have to process far too much information every day. It's worth spending an hour reading this insightful book, to reap a lifetime's worth of more efficiently handling the information deluge.

—**DAVID TETEN,** Founder of Versatile VC

Ross Dawson presents an important book for everyone who is actively looking at the future. Digital overload is a huge challenge as the sheer volume of information and content is exponentially growing, and Ross has some great pointers on dealing with it. Staying "digitally well" is crucial for future success. Read this book!

The ability to better mold one's thinking is the most powerful tool in a time of information overload, and this is an excellent road map to achieve exactly that reorientation!

Drawing on rigorous research and deep experience, Ross Dawson outlines a practical framework for reframing mindsets to thrive in a world of information overload. With our time and cognitive capacity limited, Ross provides actionable exercises, tools, profound examples, and additional resources that are transforming the way I think, work, and manage information. His Five Powers for Success are an important investment for anyone in need of strategies or a recharge for choosing how to manage overload.

This timely new book shows us how to reboot our often unhealthy relationships with information and navigate the digital era with aplomb.

I'm one of the best people in the world at thriving on overload, but this book was full of things I didn't know. I was inspired and informed by nearly every page.

You can drown in the info torrent, or surf it. Ross is your surfing guide.

How invaluable: personalizing the navigation of information abundance in the Digital Age.

THRIVING
ON
OVERLOAD

THE 5 POWERS FOR SUCCESS
IN A WORLD OF EXPONENTIAL INFORMATION

ROSS DAWSON

New York Chicago San Francisco Athens London Madrid
Mexico City Milan New Delhi Singapore Sydney Toronto

1 2 3 4 5 6 7 8 9   LCR   27 26 25 24 23 22

ISBN   978-1-264-28540-2
MHID   1-264-28540-X

e-ISBN   978-1-264-28541-9
e-MHID   1-264-28541-8

Library of Congress Cataloging-in-Publication Data

Names: Dawson, Ross, author.
Title: Thriving on overload : the five powers for success in a world of exponential
    information / Ross Dawson.
Description: New York, NY : McGraw Hill, 2022. | Includes bibliographical
    references and index.
Identifiers: LCCN 2022010053 (print) | LCCN 2022010054 (ebook) |
    ISBN 9781264285402 (hardback) | ISBN 9781264285419 (ebook)
Subjects: LCSH: Information technology—Psychological aspects. | Information
    technology—Social aspects. | Work-life balance. | Self-actualization
    (Psychology) | Stress management.
Classification: LCC HM851 .D377 2022 (print) | LCC HM851 (ebook) |
    DDC 303.48/33—dc23/eng/20220627
LC record available at https://lccn.loc.gov/2022010053
LC ebook record available at https://lccn.loc.gov/2022010054

McGraw Hill books are available at special quantity discounts to use as premiums and sales promotions or for use in corporate training programs. To contact a representative, please visit the Contact Us pages at www.mhprofessional.com.

McGraw Hill is committed to making our products accessible to all learners. To learn more about the available support and accommodations we offer, please contact us at accessibility@mheducation.com. We also participate in the Access Text Network (www.accesstext.org), and ATN members may submit requests through ATN.

To the memory of my wonderful mother, Judith Dawson,
and everyone else who has created a better world
through their kindness and warmth

CONTENTS

INTRODUCTION

Learning to Thrive

*Information is what our world runs on: the
blood and the fuel, the vital principle.*[1]

—James Gleick, author of *The Information*

n 1970, Alvin Toffler in *Future Shock* presciently anticipated
one of the central features of today's world. Toffler used the
phrase "information overload" to illustrate his broader thesis
that people were simply not able to cope with the increasing pace
of change, writing that "we are accelerating the generalized rate
of change in society. We are forcing people to adapt to a new life
pace, to confront novel situations and master them in ever shorter
intervals. We are forcing them to choose among fast-multiplying
options. We are, in other words, forcing them to process information at a far more rapid pace than was necessary in slowly evolving
societies."[2]

It was not a new concept. In his 1964 book *The Managing of
Organizations*, Bertram Gross wrote, "Information overload occurs

when the amount of input to a system exceeds its processing capacity. Decision makers have fairly limited cognitive processing capacity. Consequently, when information overload occurs, it is likely that a reduction in decision quality will occur."[3] Over a half century later, it is fair to say his prediction has been borne out.

In 1990 the genius of Tim Berners-Lee created the protocols underlying the World Wide Web. Three decades later there were over 500 billion web pages, all instantly accessible by more than 5 billion internet users around the world.[4] The same year, 64 zettabytes (that's 64 with 21 zeros after it) of data was produced, fiftyfold more than 10 years earlier.[5] If written in books stacked on top of each other, the pile would stretch to the moon and back over 300 million times.[6] The growth of information production continues to be exponential, pointing to even more staggering figures in coming years.

From that superabundance we can only ever expose ourselves to a minuscule fraction. Yet during the course of a single day in 2021 the average American consumed over 11 hours of media.[7] Two years earlier over 30 percent of the adult population (let alone teens) declared they were "almost constantly" online during their waking hours.[8] We are subjecting ourselves to close to as much information as is humanly and physically possible (though don't doubt that we will find ways to push it further).

Despite the extraordinary benefits of easy information access, for many the unwavering onslaught of news is at best wearying, and often a daily source of stress. In early 2020, 66 percent of Americans reported being "worn out" by the amount of news.[9] This sense of overwhelm is becoming pervasive around the world.

I have personally observed the global ubiquity of the phenomenon. Over the last years I have traveled to 32 countries to deliver keynotes and strategy workshops to organizations in the diverse fields of financial services, professional services, technology, media, retail, healthcare, education, government, and many others. In every case my clients expect me to understand not only the state of their industry today but also what is shaping its future, with concrete examples, as well as addressing their distinctive geographic context. To deliver value to my clients I have to keep current on a universe of information and news across an extraordinary array of domains. Perhaps it's not surprising, then, that the question I am most frequently asked at my engagements is "How on earth do you keep on top of so much information?"

In this book I will share the practices and insights I have developed through a lifetime of immersion in information. I began using the phrase "thriving on information overload" and formally researching and developing best practices in the field 25 years ago. I was designing the initial offering of my first company, helping traders and analysts in investment banks to create value from unlimited information. Since then, I have worked consistently to refine my methodologies, shaped by my work as a futurist spanning almost two decades. My approaches have served me and my clients very well and continue to help me keep abreast of the extraordinary pace of change in our world today.

I will combine these with invaluable insights I have gleaned from some of the world's most extraordinary entrepreneurs, investors, executives, professionals, authors, and researchers who appear effortlessly on top of what is happening in their industries and the world at large. I call them "information masters," those who are completely at home in a world awash with information, capable of transmuting vast mines of data into the solid gold of insight and effective action, generating success and results far beyond their peers.

What these people have in common is that they have all put in the effort required to develop five intertwined powers, distinctive capabilities that are intensely relevant in today's world of overload. We are not born with these powers; they are capacities that each one of us can build and improve. By cultivating them, we all can learn to thrive amid overwhelming excess.

Thriving on Overload starts from the premise that who we are, our identities and lives and destiny, are framed by our relationship with information. Humans exist amidst information. This includes everything we take in through our senses, now massively augmented and amplified by an explosion of content of every imaginable type. As part of our very real and necessary evolution, we must learn to flourish in today's unprecedented information-intensive world.

Perhaps the most fundamental step to thriving is to reframe our perception of our experience from one of overload to that of abundance. With abundance, we have no obligations, only choices. Shifting your mindset can allow you to experience this plenitude as joyful and liberating, treating the information landscapes we live in as places to play, to taste and savor, to appreciate as a gift completely unparalleled in human history.

The skills that you develop and the quality of your choices enable you to make the most of today's veritable cornucopia of mind fodder. This book, if you use it well, will give you those skills and choices.

The Five Powers of Thriving on Overload

In this book I will take you on a journey to explore the five powers in detail and show how you can enhance your capabilities in each of these domains, so you too can thrive. Whether you feel you are drowning in information or are already an information master, you will find perspectives, tools, and insights you can apply to improve your capabilities. The vital powers you need to prosper amid exponential change, shown in Figure I.1, are laid out in the first five chapters of this book. These five powers are inseparable. They are parts of a whole, the elemental capabilities that, when integrated, create the superpower of thriving amid excessive information.

The Power of Purpose
Living amid excess, we must make the choice to improve our relationship with information. This requires us to become clear on *why*

FIGURE I.1   The Five Powers of Thriving on Overload

we are keeping up with its ceaseless flow. Understanding our purposes for engaging with information shapes the *how* of our habits and daily practices.

There are six spheres of our life where we should consider our purpose for engaging with information: identity, expertise, ventures, society, well-being, and passions. The objective is not to come up with a fixed purpose. It is better to frame our information quests as journeys to help us refine our intentions and discover our path.

For many of us, the selection of our areas of expertise defines our career, life, and potential to contribute. As participants in society, we need to choose what news is relevant, who matters to us, and what we need to know to have a positive impact. In Chapter 1 you will consider your various purposes to guide you to an improved relationship to information and greater clarity on your path.

The Power of Framing

Any piece of information in isolation is close to meaningless. To make useful what we learn we need to form relationships, discern patterns, and build frameworks that describe the most important connections. These frames help us define a clear scope for our areas of interest and expertise, point us to where we need to be paying attention, and enable us to make sense of new ideas and information in context. Mapping our thinking dramatically accelerates knowledge development.

In Chapter 2 you will learn a range of ways to perceive and capture the links between concepts. The human brain can often best understand and process relationships visually, making visual frameworks especially useful in creating knowledge. These can be complemented by software that can capture and elucidate our thinking as it develops.

I will show you a variety of ways to create useful frameworks that help you filter information and develop refined expertise and insight. Among them is a simple process I have developed over the past 15 years for creating visual landscapes of the future, which have been invaluable in refining my own understanding and attracted many millions to view, share, and apply them.

The Power of Filtering

It is a simple fact that human cognitive capacity is limited. To find what is relevant to us we need to cast our nets wide, yet we must take care not to try to take in more than our brains can process. We need to learn to discern the information that serves us, transcending our biases and identifying the gems amid the profusion.

In Chapter 3 I will guide you through the criteria in selecting your portfolio of information portals and the sources at the core of your information habits. Choosing the best media formats for each type of content you engage with, whether they be print, text, audio, video, conversations, or more, will drive your ability to capture value.

In addition to pulling what you need toward you, we all experience excessive incoming information. Developing explicit incoming filters and communicating these clearly can help limit how much you need to sift through each day.

The Power of Attention

We know we need to pay attention to what matters and not let ourselves be distracted by what doesn't. Yet attention is not a single thing that you either have or don't have. Sometimes we need to be completely focused, diving deep to distill insights from dense sources and develop mental frameworks. At other times we need to explore, seeking specific information we require. Serendipity, the faculty of encountering happy accidents, is in fact often not chance at all. We can develop the skill of intentionally creating the conditions for felicitous connections with new ideas. We also need to understand that our attention is a finite resource; we can learn how to regenerate our capacity for focus. I will teach you the six different attention modes you need to distill value from information.

In Chapter 4 you will learn how to develop information routines that give you what you need to achieve your objectives without overwhelming you, as well as a set of practices to improve your capacity for attention, a foundational skill for success in a world of overload.

The Power of Synthesis

Synthesis—connecting and integrating disparate concepts—is the most distinctive human faculty. Its value is being amplified as the rise of artificial intelligence supplants many of our other capabilities. Only from the continuing act of sense-making and synthesis are we able to truly comprehend our chosen domains of expertise, perceive emerging opportunities, and make effective decisions in our work and personal lives.

In Chapter 5 I will help you build a wellspring of the elements that support our capacity for synthesis. At the foundation is openness to ideas, an attribute that confers powerful advantage in an accelerating world. We will learn other vital abilities, such as creatively perceiving connections to enrich the mental models that are at the heart of our thinking. The ultimate outcome of our enhanced capability of synthesis is making better decisions and more successfully creating the outcomes we desire.

Chapter 6, the final chapter, consolidates the lessons of the five core chapters. It looks forward to the opportunities as well as the challenges of how information excess will evolve in coming years. The reality is our brains are evolving; we have the choice to make them better suited to the world of today and tomorrow.

Integrating the Paradoxes

Thriving on a surfeit of information is not something you can boil down to a set of simple steps to follow. If it were that easy, everyone could do it. In fact, you must reconcile many sets of what appear to be contradictory imperatives. You need to focus tightly and also scan broadly, delve into molecular detail yet see the big picture, develop clarity and acknowledge uncertainty, analyze into components and synthesize them into a whole, apply both rationality and intuition, be highly discriminating and also wide open to new information.

Astronomer and science communicator Carl Sagan observed, "It seems to me what is called for is an exquisite balance between two conflicting needs: the most skeptical scrutiny of all hypotheses that are served up to us and at the same time a great openness to new ideas."[10]

Neuroscientist and philosopher Iain McGilchrist in his cerebral bestseller *The Master and His Emissary* explores the complementary roles of the "exploratory attention" of the brain's left hemisphere and the "narrow attention" of the right hemisphere.[11] He posits that all knowledge entails cycling from the broad purview of the left hemisphere to the detailed apprehension of the right hemisphere, and then back to generate a comprehensive view. Our dance between perceiving minutiae and a holistic understanding of the world must encompass both. Neither is meaningful without the other.

Acknowledging and integrating these many paradoxes under-lies our ability to excel across all the five powers. Throughout the book I will return to this vital theme to help weave together the powers into a whole, a set of capabilities that together are far more than the sum of their parts.

How to Read This Book

The primary intention of this book is to be useful to you, to help you thrive in a frenzied world, to enhance your information habits and routines to enable you to have a richer and more successful life.

In these pages you will find my advice on reading books, which of course also applies here. I suggest that you read the opening section (as you have), then spend perhaps 15 to 30 minutes skim-ming all the way through, looking at section headers, diagrams, and any immediately intriguing passages to get a sense of the book as a whole. I have written the book to be read from start to finish, but feel free to dive first into any sections you think may prove particularly useful for you. Read at the pace that best suits you, slowing where you think you can derive the most value, and speed-ing ahead through sections you don't find as compelling.

For the lessons in this book to be of value, you need to put them into practice. At the conclusion of every chapter, you will find exercises to apply for yourself the ideas you have encoun-tered. Taken together, the exercises will help you build a personal "information strategy" that will make you more effective in your information habits and routines. The exercises will help you develop your capabilities in all five powers: in Chapter 1 to define your relationship with information and understand your *why*; in Chapter 2 to start developing useful frameworks; in Chapter 3 to select your portfolio of information portals; in Chapter 4 to design effective information routines; in Chapter 5 to enhance your abil-ities at synthesis; and in Chapter 6 to set a personal information action plan. I strongly encourage you to do the exercises, whether you feel you are early in your journey or already proficient. Even the slightest improvement in your information capabilities will reap you rich rewards.

It would of course not make sense for this book to be excessively long, adding to your already substantial information burden. With the aim of making the book both as useful and as succinct as possible, at the end of the book I have provided a curated and annotated compilation of resources for those who wish to dive deeper, including lists of further reading, podcasts, educational courses, and apps. Extensive additional resources are also available at thrivingonoverload.com, including a podcast of all of the interviews for this book, downloadable exercise sheets, software reviews, an in-depth online course, and far more.

Learning to Thrive

Humans are intrinsically information-voracious animals. This has served us well as we have developed cities, civilizations, and technologies over the years, always building on the achievements of our predecessors.

We have created extraordinary technologies, including medical advances, remarkable materials, new sources of energy, and improved forms of transportation, by consistently drawing on developments around the world as they have emerged. Yet the heart of our progress, supporting and interwoven through all our other technologies, has been in information technologies, which have progressed at an exponential pace for decades.

These developments have wrought a world in which the perverse punishment for our hubris is a superabundance of information with the potential to drown us.

I believe that we all have a fundamental choice on whether we learn to thrive on overload—by experiencing it as abundance—rather than allowing it to overwhelm us. You and I happen to have been born in a time of unprecedented change and an explosion in the creation and accessibility of information. Each of us can decide whether we will treat this reality as a problem or an opportunity.

I invite you to dive into this book and use it to enhance the capabilities that will allow you not just to cope with today's massive information overload, but to thrive on it, to prosper and succeed as never before, using these skills to create a better life for yourself and those around you.

CHAPTER 1

THE POWER OF PURPOSE

Know Why

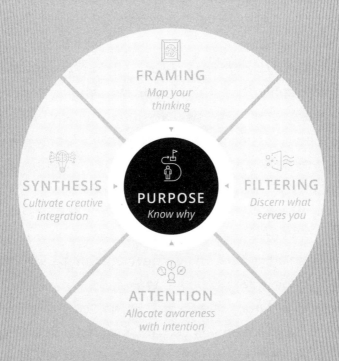

FRAMING
Map your thinking

SYNTHESIS
Cultivate creative integration

PURPOSE
Know why

FILTERING
Discern what serves you

ATTENTION
Allocate awareness with intention

In a world deluged by irrelevant information, clarity is power.[1]

**—Yuval Noah Harari,
author of *21 Lessons for the 21st Century***

Humans' singular propensity for novelty means we are continually distracted by the new and shiny. Yet we have the ability to build an increasingly positive relationship with information. Understanding our purpose for engaging with information, the *why*, allows us to design the *how* of our information habits.

We can apply this in six important spheres of our lives and work: identity, expertise, ventures, society, well-being, and passions. For each, we need to follow a journey in which our purpose guides how we engage with information, and the information we find helps us clarify our intentions.

As we develop our capabilities in each sphere, we need to focus first on establishing foundational knowledge and then on keeping current on new developments. Each of these requires distinct information strategies.

Living in a torrent of information, don't try to drink from the firehose more than you can or want. Balancing your purposes so you only undertake the achievable is the key to turning crippling overload into enabling abundance.

The objective of this book is not to help you find your life's purpose. It is to help you thrive in a world in which information is the very essence of our lives and livelihoods. Yet the indispensable first step to live amid superabundance without getting lost is to be conscious about what you want in your work and life. Only this will allow you to understand the role of information in your life, discern what information is and isn't relevant to you, and engage with information in the most productive way possible.

We each have a relationship with information, just as we have a relationship with money, food, and all the people in our lives, those we love and those we do not. The quality of our relationships is reflected in our mindsets, attitudes, emotions, and behaviors— in this case about our interactions with information. These can be positive and enabling, manifesting curiosity, joy of learning, desire to improve, drive to contribute, and sufficiency. Or they can be destructive, reflecting overwhelm, anxiety, guilt, or dread of boredom. As we understand these dynamics, we can learn to shape a better relationship with information.

Improving your relationship with information is at the heart of creating success and balance in your life.

Our brains' ancient physiology makes this far harder than we would like. The first land animals developed a brain structure to help them forage for their daily diet. These foraging behaviors, based on the reward mechanism of dopamine, are in fact close to mathematically optimal strategies.[2] As primates and then humans evolved, primitive brain structures such as the basal ganglia were complemented by more complex structures, including our prefrontal cortex, enabling even more refined seeking capabilities. Despite our dramatically more sophisticated cognitive abilities, the pleasure from dopamine that rewards seeking remains at the center of humans' goal-directed behavior.

In the quest to understand our singular propensity for information, researchers proposed the idea of "information foraging." They noted that "humans actively seek, gather, share, and consume information to a degree unapproached by other organisms." Drawing on the science of food foraging, they found that precisely the same dopamine reward mechanisms apply to how we deal with information.[3]

Now that most of us can eat as much as we want, our in-built penchant for sweet, fatty foods has led to over half of all adults in developed countries being overweight or obese.[4] In a similar vein, with unlimited information always at our fingertips, our dopamine-driven proclivity for novelty is effectively insatiable, leading most people to deeply unhealthy information habits.

Humans are best understood as information-processing animals. It is our nature to seek, make sense of the world, and invent. Our craving for information is a profound blessing, having generated all human progress. Yet it can also be a curse if we succumb to its darker manifestations. How we deal with our powerful predilections in a world of unlimited information ultimately defines our life.

> *You ARE the information you consume.*
> *Your choice of the information you take in*
> *determines whether you become who YOU*
> *want to be or who others want you to be.*

In a society centered on information, the odds of feeling in control of our information habits are heavily stacked against us. As recently as 2007, the top 10 companies in the world by market capitalization included only one information technology company, Microsoft. In 2021, 8 of the top 10 were technology firms, and this is only if you don't include Berkshire Hathaway, whose largest stock holding is Apple, and self-driving car company Tesla.

This leads to an economy in which "you are the product," or more precisely, your attention is the most valuable asset. The most sophisticated and technologically advanced companies on the planet are spending billions of dollars to refine their ability to hijack your awareness. Given our brains' propensity to constantly seek information, the default outcome is that our focus is always pulled to the latest enticing tidbit, and the information that enters our minds is largely what media, social media, and marketers want us to take in. But it need not be this way. We have the power to choose who we are and how we deal with information.

You need a reference point so you can make the choices throughout every day of which information you allow in. Understanding your purpose for engaging with information is a prerequisite for thriving amid excess. It is the foundation for developing and applying each of the other powers you will learn in this book.

We all have our own reasons for engaging with information. We might want to make a good living, fulfill our curiosity, build high-potential ventures, keep current on the state of our nation, learn about fascinating topics, invest successfully, have a positive impact on the world, or simply entertain ourselves. Everyone has their own desires and objectives.

You need to clearly understand your purpose for engaging with information, the WHY, to shape your relationship with information, the HOW of your habits and daily practices.

The word *purpose* comes with a lot of baggage, as at every turn self-help gurus exhort us to find our purpose in life. Yet whether or not we have discovered "the reason we were born," we all have intentions that drive our actions through every day. Engaging with information in its myriad forms comprises the bulk of our waking lives, so knowing why we are doing it is essential for our information odysseys to benefit us rather than lead us astray.

Clarifying your intentions allows you to better define the relationship with information that will best serve you. Your information habits should be shaped by your unique priorities.

There are six primary spheres that define most people's relationship with information, as shown in Figure 1.1. We have multiple purposes, rather than just one. Throughout this chapter we will explore how you can uncover your intentions, with the sole objective of helping you to engage more usefully with information. Don't assume these six spheres are necessarily the most relevant for everyone. You might consider other domains more important. The exercises at the end of this chapter will help you reflect on what is most meaningful to you.

FIGURE 1.1 Six Spheres to Define Your Relationship with Information

Through the following four chapters we will examine *how* to enact a positive relationship with information. This chapter aims to help you understand your *why*. Knowing why you engage with information is necessary to achieve your unique objectives.

It is critical to recognize that your purpose, your why for engaging with information, is not a constant. You are changing, and the world in which you live is transforming at a pace that you can interpret as either exciting or terrifying. In fact, one of the most important reasons to be aware of news, developments, and emerging insights is that they allow you to clarify and evolve how you think about your path.

Make your life a virtuous cycle of applying your purpose to uncovering information and using the information you encounter to refine your purpose.

Learning helps us recognize what we want to learn. This applies to every sphere of our engagement with information, and to the elements that help us define an enabling relationship with information. Where it is most pointed is in developing the most central of the six spheres: our identity, our understanding of ourselves, who we wish to be, and our place in society.

Identity

Have you ever doubted the trajectory of your life? I dearly hope so. The only way to find your path is through a process of discovery, which by its nature means sometimes (or often) going off track, and then realizing it.

There were numerous times in my career when I doubted not just my path, but myself. At those times I had good jobs with prospects, but I and my work—or more often, my working environment—were evidently far from a perfect fit. I later described myself as at times feeling like "a fish out of water." I questioned whether I was in the right place to create the life I desired. As I wondered whether I could find the right path for me, there were moments when I struggled and considered whether I might live a very ordinary life.

Even after I had launched my own business and more than ever directed my own fate, it wasn't always apparent how to be true to myself. After my first book on knowledge-based relationships came out, many professional firms asked me to work with them on developing their key client programs and coaching their senior relationship executives. I believed strongly in the value of my work, but it wasn't what most inspired me. Given the extent of corporate demand, I could have stopped there and developed a significant business in the space, but I was tantalized by my dream of becoming a full-time futurist, so I established an entirely new company to help leaders better see and create the future. On my journey, by dint of essaying many, many possibilities and paths, the arc of my life has become far clearer, though it absolutely remains one of ongoing discovery.

"I know who I am when I see what I do," is how management professor Herminia Ibarra puts it.[5] Our life's journey is one of trying things to see what works for us. That is how we uncover what we're good at and what brings us satisfaction or even joy.

> *If you can see your path laid out in front of you step by step, you know it's not your path. Your own path you make with every step you take. That's why it's your path.*[6]
>
> **—Joseph Campbell**

If you have crystal clarity on what you wish to achieve in your life and the positive impact you wish to have on the world, you are blessed. It makes it far easier to filter information, as it is evident what is germane to your intentions and what can be ignored. You can focus utterly on the ventures that will fulfill your raison d'être.

However, for the vast majority of people, finding their identity and purpose is a lifelong journey.

At the age of six, Jacqueline Novogratz decided she wanted to change the world. But she didn't know how. She started her working career as a banker, only because it afforded her the opportunity to travel the world. As she worked in Latin America she was enticed by the color and vibrancy of the slums, meeting inspiring community businesspeople who didn't use or trust banks. Inspired by this unmet need, she established a microfinance organization in Rwanda, moving past deep struggles to eventually found the global nonprofit Acumen. Her organization has invested over $100 million in transformative social enterprises that have helped over 300 million very low-income people.[7]

Speaking to a graduating class, Novogratz said, "We want simple answers, clear pathways to success. . . . Life does not work that way. And instead of looking for answers all the time, my wish for you is that you get comfortable living the questions."[8]

If you recognize it for what it is, the quest to find your path can be as fulfilling as eventually finding it, for all its frustrations. It means you can and should be exploring more diversely, to uncover what resonates for you.

Curiosity is an intrinsic motivation, central to all human progress and learning. I believe deeply that the pursuit of knowledge for knowledge's sake is a worthy human motivation, with as a wonderful bonus generating the most valuable innovation.[9] To discover yourself, simply pursue what you find most fascinating.

If you are seeking to clarify your purpose and directions, that gives you license and motivation to explore more broadly than those who feel they have already defined their intent for their lives. Your adventures in information and ideas can feed your process of finding where you are called to invest your energy.

Whether you are close to certain or have almost no idea, try to state your life's purpose as well as you can. It doesn't matter if it doesn't feel quite right. Treat it as a placeholder, one you intend to replace when you find something more compelling. You will find that even a tentative idea of your purpose immediately clarifies what information will support you and what behaviors will lead to the fulfillment of your purpose. Consider your information adventures as a voyage of refining your identity and life's purpose.

Expertise

The single decision that will most shape your daily information habits is the choice of your area of expertise. As human knowledge progresses exponentially, there is only one way to keep up: select tightly defined domains in which you will develop profound knowledge. If you have too broad an ambit, others who are more focused will inevitably surge ahead of you. Selecting and developing your fields of expertise are necessarily at the center, not just of your career, but also of your relationship to information.

When Chris Anderson, at the time editor in chief of *Wired* magazine, succumbed to his passion to establish drone company 3D Robotics in 2009, he knew exactly who he wanted as his cofounder. He had recently set up an enthusiasts' message board, DIY Drones, where Jordi Muñoz was sharing his profound knowledge of the realities of building drones. "He was just ahead of us all," says Anderson.[10] It turned out Muñoz had joined the forum as a teenager in Tijuana, Mexico. By focusing all of his energy and intellect, he had made himself into what he calls a "Google PhD," a self-taught world-leading expert in this fascinating emerging technology, and soon president of a rapidly growing drone company.[11]

Some people proclaim themselves to be generalists. That is a very tough gig in an accelerating world. You have to earn the right to be a generalist, and the only path is through being a specialist. To understand the world at large, you need to have built a deep understanding of probably not just one domain, but several, so you can understand the linkages and connections, how they all fit together. I think I can fairly claim to be a generalist, but that is based on having worked in many roles in many industries in many countries over many years, along the way spending numerous extended periods developing specialist expertise in diverse areas.

That said, we need more than single-domain expertise. The corollary of intensifying specialization is that we must also excel at collaboration. Any specialization on its own has limited value. In an increasingly complex and interdependent world, the value of depth comes from its relationship to other disciplines and domains. To collaborate well, we need to have an understanding of other fields. The most productive entrepreneurs, executives, and scientists are voracious in the breadth of their interests to complement their area of singular focus. Patrick Collison, billionaire founder of payments company Stripe, is an omnivorous reader, devouring books on science, history, society, health, spirituality, economics, philosophy, technology, and biographies as well as business and classic literature.[12]

Top employers such as management consultants McKinsey & Company have long sought people with "T-shaped" skills, combining depth and breadth. In a complex world it can be useful to choose more than one area of expertise, to develop what are called "pi-shaped" skills. The shape of the Greek letter pi (π) suggests two domains for depth—the legs of the symbol—to complement the breadth of the top bar, instead of the singular focus of T-shaped people. While dividing your attention inevitably attenuates the depth you can attain, in an intensely interconnected world there is immense value to understanding complementary domains such as science and art, business and technology, design and coding, or many more specific pairings. As author Robert Greene says, "The future belongs to those who learn more skills and combine them in creative ways."[13]

Selecting your areas of expertise is a lifelong journey. If you are going to dedicate much of your life to developing deep knowledge, you want to be not just interested in the topic, but captivated, thrilled to immerse yourself even if there were no reward. The more you learn, the further your interest will develop. When you select an area of expertise to focus on, assess not only current demand but also future potential, and over time monitor for signals of how its value may evolve. Helping your children to select their fields of study and work must take into account that some jobs will disappear and others will emerge, and the fact that your offspring too will blossom in surprising and sometimes wonderful ways.

Given its central role in your life and career, you need to be highly conscious in choosing your expertise and the breadth that complements it. Start by articulating your current positioning and direction. Always be open to evolving your chosen expertise, or even shifting to a completely new domain. Your knowledge, and especially the skills you acquired in developing it, will serve you well whatever you do next. As you go through the rest of the book, consider in precisely what domain you wish to become a world-class (or world-leading) expert, and design your information habits accordingly.

Ventures

In 2006 Facebook hired 23-year-old Jeff Hammerbacher out of Wall Street to establish its data analysis team, which would prove central to the burgeoning social network's success. Hammerbacher later left Facebook to found data platform company Cloudera, which grew far beyond his expectations to be valued at over $1 billion in a matter of years.

Hammerbacher literally invented the term "data science" but found himself disappointed with how these incredibly powerful skills were being applied, ruefully observing that "the best minds of my generation are thinking about how to make people click ads. That sucks."[14] He yearned to turn his capabilities to a field he truly cared about. He thought that biomedicine was a field where it would be useful to apply data science and where he "probably won't get bored." Exposing himself more to the field confirmed his interest. A friend who had recently been appointed to run the Department of Genetics at Mount Sinai Health System helped create a position for him to explore data science applications in healthcare.

Hammerbacher had zero formal education in the space and a massive amount to learn, so as a self-professed autodidact, he set out to teach himself what he needed to know. He focused on reading textbooks and in particular review papers, which consolidate the research in a field, as well as setting up conversations with the most interesting people in the field to help frame his understanding.

"Review papers are key for me," Hammerbacher says. "Finding a good review paper on a topic, and then figuring out who wrote it and then what their recent research is, and just finding kindred spirits, people who think like you do and being able to converse with them and interactively map a domain."[15] Establishing a broad knowledge of the field has led Hammerbacher to found and invest in a range of promising healthcare startups. He continues to push out the boundaries of health data and cancer immunotherapy, having coauthored 20 research papers.

In the initial stages of a venture, be it a high-potential startup or a local community initiative, you need to focus on framing your understanding with matching information strategies. As you grasp the essentials of the space, your relationship with information shifts to one of being consistently alert for relevant changes in your environment and emerging opportunities.

*Success in ventures requires first foundational
knowledge and then consistently
keeping abreast of change.*

The more precisely you can define your venture's ambitions in terms of scope and impact, the better you can shape your relationship with information. What are the theses or assumptions on which your venture is based? In what industry sector or geography will you play? What social or other nonfinancial outcomes would you like to flow from the success of your business? Your responses to these kinds of questions will help determine information relevance.

When Jeff Bezos founded Amazon.com in 1996, his long-term aspirations meant that he closely followed every aspect of the flourishing ecommerce space, not just the book industry where the company commenced.

Society

"It isn't that I don't like current events. There have just been so many of them lately," reflects a delightful cartoon in Marshall McLuhan's book, *The Medium Is the Massage*, published well over 50 years ago.[16]

Indeed, most people want to keep current with developments, despite the daily onslaught. To participate fully in society, we need to be informed on the state of the world. Only this allows us to have grounded opinions on what might create a better community, nation, and world, and how we can best contribute, if we choose. We need to pay attention to what will lead us to understand the society we live in. Where possible we want to hear directly from people's everyday experiences. However, we must inevitably, very carefully and selectively, draw on mainstream news media.

It is an instructive exercise to consider in depth why you want to see the news at all, and how it affords you a better life. Understanding our personal motivations is necessary to shape the most positive relationship possible with news. Is it so you can participate in your democracy through informed voting or voicing your opinion? Is it to have intelligent conversations about the state of the world with your friends? Do you want to know what can help your community? Are you simply curious about the state of humanity? At a time when many people's relationship with news is highly dysfunctional, clarifying your intentions lets you adopt behaviors that best serve your purpose.

*Be clear on what you want from news to
transcend what news wants from you.*

Philosopher Alain de Botton notes that "the news wants you to keep reading, but you also know there are times you should stop. The news is the best distraction ever invented. It sounds so serious and important. But it wants you never to have any free time ever again, time where you can daydream, unpack your anxieties and have a conversation with yourself."[17] Building a better relationship with news starts with understanding why you spend the time.

For many, some kinds of news are directly relevant to their work and the development of their expertise. Anyone who is seeking to have impact at scale needs a broad understanding of the state of society. This can entail following local, national, or international affairs, business, and social developments. However, this rarely requires frequent refreshes.

Those who work in media or politics need to keep constantly updated, but for most of us it is a huge time sink. The benefit of getting updates throughout the day as opposed to daily or even less often is minimal compared with the time investment. In shaping our relationship with news, we need to consider not just what news we want to engage with, but also how often.

Presuming that our life objectives include living a happy and healthy life, we need to acknowledge the mental health impact of overengaging with news. We all know that reported news is almost unmitigatedly negative; good news is rarely as exciting and click-worthy. Waking up to a barrage of pessimism every day inevitably shapes our outlook on life. Media analyst Thomas Baekdal observes that "the more you look at this, the more you realize that the way we do news today is seriously harmful to people's mental health."[18] We need to be deliberate in how we engage.

To be well informed on the state of society you need to go far beyond the headlines, the latest political machinations, and tawdry stories that entice prurient interest. Seek insight into the behaviors of those from different generations or nations, uncover the different perspectives leading to conflicts, look for the incisive social perspectives so often expressed in the latest in arts and culture.

Take a step back and consider your place in the world. How much do you want to and need to know about what is going on? Why do you want to be informed? What are the highest priorities for you? Realize that it is all too easy to get sucked into the news vortex. Decide what will genuinely add value to your life and support your ability to participate in and contribute to a better society.

Well-Being

Undoubtedly the most direct impact of human progress we have experienced stems from advances in healthcare. Over the past century life expectancy has increased by over 30 years in most developed countries. Now that we have found ways to treat most common illnesses, many individuals and (hopefully) institutions are shifting attention from how to manage maladies to how to increase well-being and potential. An explosion of resources and information helps us on that path.

Fitness and health trackers have added massively to the personal information available to us. Many people monitor their time exercising, number of steps taken, heart rates, sleep patterns, and a wealth of other data, with some also tracking food and supplement intake, posture, and much more in seeking to improve their performance. If we use it well, this information can lead to immense positive change.

When speaker and author Chris Dancy turned 40, he had never eaten a salad, orange, or slice of watermelon. He weighed close to 300 pounds, on an average day eating 3,000 to 4,000 calories, drinking 30 Diet Cokes, and smoking two packs of cigarettes. Already avidly tracking his personal data, he dug deeper and found a correlation: he rarely smoked when he was drinking water, helping him drive down his smoking. He identified the specific types of exercise that had the most positive impact and the times of day they were most helpful. Dancy continued to dig into what behaviors drove improvements in his health. Five years later, having learned through data how best to adopt positive habits, he achieved his target weight of 175 pounds, in the process becoming vegan and giving up cigarettes.[19] Information alone does not change us. We need to focus on learning what drives and shifts our behaviors.

Framing our relationship with well-being information begins by understanding *who* we care for and what we can do to help. How do you want to improve your health or potential? Are there loved ones you want to support?

Well-being goes far beyond health concerns. Our relationship with health information should be shaped by considering what will help us or others live the best possible life. Our emotional states, our social life, the cleanliness of our homes, our spiritual practices, the entertainment we choose, are all central aspects of our quality of life.

Our well-being includes not just our body, but also our circumstances, including our finances. As with other aspects of our well-being, we need to engage with information about both our own situation and the external environment: the fundamentals of personal finances or investment, where investment opportunities lie, tax implications, and more.

Our relationship with financial information can be fraught. If you have a family budget, checking whether your spending is on track at least every few days can be very useful, whereas daily updates on the state of an investment you intend to keep for the long term is not helpful. Unless you are a finance professional, avoid investments that require active monitoring. They can be enormous drains on your attention, and it is impossible to outperform those whose livelihoods allow utter focus on the markets.

Spend time to define the well-being outcomes you seek for yourself or others. Do you want to learn what will improve an ailment? Do you want to feel positive and happy throughout the day? Do you wish to reach an ideal weight to look and feel great? Do you want to improve your sports performance or even win an Olympic medal? Do you want to be sharp and focused to excel at your work or business? Consider the best way to engage with information to support your objectives.

Passions

David Solomon's demanding job as CEO of storied investment bank Goldman Sachs doesn't consume his whole life. He has a side gig as a DJ mixing electronic dance music, playing at popular festivals and boasting over 700,000 monthly listeners on his Spotify channel.[20] His passion requires him to keep on top of the latest music releases, scouring new releases and mixes to be current in rapidly evolving music fashion. The thrill of performing to a pulsing audience is founded on absorbing information of a quite different nature than that required in his day job.

We all have passions that transcend our work lives. For many, sports are a defining interest, in some cases leading to obsessive poring over statistics and the manifold potential predictors of team performance. Others choose to follow the lives and fortunes of musicians, movie stars, or other celebrities, the latest in art or theater, or indulge in more specialist interests such as train or plane spotting, or collecting stamps, period furniture, classic dolls, or any of a universe of possible interests.

Any of these passions drives a quest to be informed of the latest or to develop deeper understanding. These fascinations are deeply human—they fulfill intrinsic needs. Having diverse interests make us more well-rounded than those who focus too narrowly. We need to acknowledge that extracurricular interests beyond our work, studies, and ventures need to be balanced with our other information priorities. Yet for many they are absolutely part of a healthy information diet, in following what intrigues us and absorbs our attention.

Acknowledge your interests and obsessions that require information. Hiking or going fishing doesn't need much. Collecting contemporary art or following sports, for example, does. Consider what information will most support your enjoyment, its place in your broader information habits, and the time and attention you should dedicate relative to your other purposes.

In the Flow

To slake your thirst beside a torrential river, you don't try to drink the whole river. You dip in a cup and take a sip. You might endeavor to fill your container with the best quality water from the stream, but you don't attempt to drink more than you need. It wouldn't make you feel better, and it is in any case completely impossible to take in more than a tiny fraction of the flow.

We are finite beings living amid infinite information. Even though our brains are the most extraordinary natural phenomenon from the known universe's profusion of wonders, our cognition is severely restricted. However much we may want to soak in more information, our biology has hard limits. It is not useful to attempt the impossible; we need to acknowledge and work within our brains' constraints.

In the words of poet Rumi, "Life is a balance between holding on and letting go." For our relationship to information to be enabling rather than destructive, we need to gracefully accept our limitations.

Letting go of trying to keep up transforms crippling overload into enabling abundance.

We are multifaceted beings, with priorities across work, family, community, health, and beyond, all of which require information to accomplish. When you consider your many purposes, you will likely find you are setting yourself up to try to do more than is reasonable, or perhaps even possible. You have choices to make.

"Annual income twenty pounds, annual expenditure nineteen and six, result happiness. Annual income twenty pounds, annual expenditure twenty pounds ought and six, result misery," wrote Charles Dickens in his great novel *David Copperfield*. As for money, also for information. Trying to do even slightly more than you can creates an immediate feeling of overwhelm. In contrast, maintaining your intentions for information intake a fraction less than what is realistic generates a sense of liberation.

Whatever your purposes are in life, they will be furthered by a constructive relationship with information. Central to achieving that is simply understanding your relative priorities, allocating your time accordingly, and not undertaking more than is possible.

Amplifying the Power of Purpose

This chapter has offered a framework for you to clarify your intentions across the major domains of your life. Take the time to reflect on these. You will be amply repaid by any effort you spend developing a positive, enabling relationship with the information that is at the heart of your work and life.

In coming chapters, you will apply your evolving apprehension of your intentions. In Chapter 2 you will learn how to frame and develop your understanding of your priority topics; in Chapter 3 you will develop filtering criteria based on your objectives; while in Chapter 4 you will create information routines that embed your priorities in your daily schedule.

EXERCISES

Purpose

What are your current best articulations of your life's purpose, your intentions of what you wish to achieve, that will help define your engagement with information?

The Priority Spheres of Your Life

In this chapter I suggested six spheres to consider your relationship with information. Perhaps there are other spheres of your life that are important to you; if so, add those to the list that follows.

For each, indicate the relative importance. Don't try to allocate more than 100 percent of your attention. If something is more important, then you have to reduce from other spheres. Go on to consider for each sphere one action or habit that could improve your outcomes. Come back to this after you have learned techniques from the rest of the book.

Sphere	Proportion of Your Attention (% to add up to 100)	What Is One Thing You Can Do to Improve Your Relationship with Information in This Sphere?
Identity		
Expertise		
Ventures		
Well-being		
Society		
Passions		

Your Expertise

Consider your current and potential future expertise. For each domain assess your current level of expertise on a scale of 1 to 10 to help gauge what may be required to develop it.

	Area of Expertise	Current Level of Expertise
What are your current areas of expertise?		
What areas of expertise could best support your purpose and objectives?		
Where will you focus on developing breadth?		
What might your expertise be in 3 to 5 years?		
What might your expertise be in 10+ years?		

CHAPTER 2

THE POWER OF FRAMING

Map Your Thinking

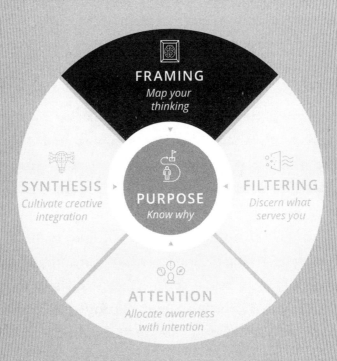

Faced with information overload, we have no alternative but to pattern-recognition.[1]

—Marshall McLuhan, media visionary and author of *The Medium Is the Massage*

Information is only meaningful in context. To enhance our expertise, understanding, and ability to make good decisions, we need to develop the power of framing. This entails building concept frameworks or maps that help us perceive connections and make sense of new information.

Visual frameworks are invaluable in helping us form and recognize the patterns that are the foundation of expertise. The three primary structures for mapping knowledge are trees, networks, and systems, with associated visualization techniques including mind maps, concept maps, and systems diagrams, respectively.

We can build rich frameworks of our knowledge through connected note-taking on index cards and in software, as well as through writing, often in conjunction with visual representations. Structured thinking about the future can provide a useful reference for filtering and sensitizing ourselves to what is relevant.

n 1992, coinciding with the emergence of the World Wide Web, analyst Jerry Michalski was named editor of *Release 1.0*, the highly influential newsletter on the digital economy established by technology ventures doyen Esther Dyson. Michalski's job was to cover what was hot in the swiftly expanding online and digital world, immersing him in fast-paced change and constant approaches from startup entrepreneurs wanting to pitch their ideas to him.

Six years into his role, helping his clients make sense of the heady early days of the commercial internet, Michalski began working on a feature on the nascent field of online bookmarking, and was approached by Harlan Hugh, the founder of a company called TheBrain. Michalski was skeptical of the name and their concept, but he accepted a meeting. Their conversation changed Michalski's life. In Hugh's product he saw a way not just to capture all the information he came across, but a means to connect all the sources to create a multidimensional map of the concepts.

"It turns out that this piece of software was exactly how my brain worked," says Michalski. "I wrote about them, I invited them to our conference, and I started using their software, not knowing that 23 years later I would be curating the same data file that I started the very first day I started using it."[2]

He shares his curated and deeply interlinked collection of content and links with anyone who cares to take a look, making it the largest public "brain" in the world. It can be found at jerrysbrain .com, assembling well over 400,000 resources connected in a rich lattice, providing deep insights into how he thinks for his own benefit as well as for others.

"I've got like the world's largest puzzle in how the world works. I'm busy snapping little pieces in place, which gives me a little oxytocin hit, which causes the lather, rinse, repeat kind of addiction response to kick in. So, the time that other people would spend putting a link in a spreadsheet or somewhere, I add a link to this one curated mind map."

Michalski's life is an ongoing process of building a framework that connects all the relevant, interesting information he comes across, enabling him to easily find whatever he is looking for, and helping him develop both deep expertise and expansive understanding of the world.

Building personal frameworks to connect the information and ideas you encounter is a foundational power in a world of overload. Let us investigate some of the approaches to framing that you can adopt to amplify your knowledge and expertise.

Concept Frameworks

Any piece of information alone is essentially meaningless. To be useful it requires a frame of reference: it needs to be set in context of the rich array of data, concepts, and ideas that make up our current understanding of the world.

These are our "mental models": the way we represent the world in our mind, our understanding of how things work. Built on the totality of how we have made sense of our life's experience, they shape every decision we make and action we take.

Later in this book we will examine how we can enhance our mental models to be as effective as possible in a fast-changing world. In this chapter we will delve into how to build the "concept frameworks" that link a universe of ideas to formulate valuable knowledge. Judiciously connecting ideas is the foundation of building more useful mental models and making sense of a complex world.

Concept frameworks provide the bedrock
on which to build real intelligence.

Creating frameworks vastly accelerates our development of expertise and deepens our understanding. It allows us to assess new information, see where it fits and doesn't fit, and evolve our understanding and expertise so we can take better action.

Maps to Chart the Future

Tim O'Reilly avowedly built his publishing business O'Reilly Media to provide "the picks and shovels of learning to the Silicon Valley gold rush," uncovering emerging trends and supplying information resources to the startups seeking to mine those seams. A cover story in *Inc.* magazine described O'Reilly as "the oracle of Silicon Valley," noting that "he has been on top of nearly every important technology development of the past three decades."[3] O'Reilly believes his ability to see trends ahead of others is founded on building frameworks—which he calls maps—to connect his thinking.

"I think of myself as a mapmaker," he says. He considers maps to be "an aid to seeing," sensitizing you to trends and how they are unfolding.[4] "A lot of the work that I've done over the years has simply been trying to construct a map by looking around," he says.[5] The maps have many elements, some already in place and some that might not even exist yet. Connecting the pieces of the puzzle allows O'Reilly to recognize what fits and generate deeper understanding. "You go, oh, there's the piece that was missing," he says. "You lock it in place, and everything starts to make sense."[6]

This kind of thinking is not created in a moment; it emerges from finding and connecting ideas over an extended period. Referring to his prescient vision of the rise of software as a service (SaaS), O'Reilly notes that "it had taken years to explore the landscape sufficiently to fill in all the blank spaces."[7]

Frameworks or maps generate understanding by capturing the conceptual connections we see, which in turn help us see other important relationships. They are not just tools for sense-making; they also help us improve how we filter, allocate our attention, and develop useful knowledge.

Creating Knowledge

Information and knowledge are not the same thing. Information simply informs you of facts; it does not tell you what you need to do. Knowledge is the capacity to act effectively.[8] An ongoing process of sense-making is required to transform all your experience and learning into useful capabilities.

As we are sucked into today's unremitting torrents of information, one of the greatest risks is not being able to pull back to see the big picture. We need perspective so we can make sense of the deluge, form linkages, comprehend the import, and generate the insights that will help us to achieve our objectives.

Our intention should not be to master the tide of information. That aim would imperil us toward becoming lost in the abyss of unremitting updates. Our task is to develop useful knowledge, comprehend the nature of what we are working on, and accurately predict the results of our actions. In short, we are striving to understand the world. To do this our minds must form and recognize patterns.

Pattern Recognition and Pattern Formation

As a boy Herbert Simon went in a group picking wild strawberries on Washington Island in Lake Michigan. All the children quickly filled their pails, but Simon could find only a few. He had to be told that strawberries were red and leaves were green. He couldn't tell the difference; he had discovered he was color-blind.[9] He had learned a powerful lesson: that the world we see is not what is actually there, not only for those with achromatic vision.

Simon commenced as a promising undergraduate at the University of Chicago studying economics. Then, to avoid the requirement of taking an accounting course, he joined the political science department, which at the time specialized in behavioral science. Simon determined that he would focus his efforts on "the phenomena of human thinking and problem solving as the essential core of both organizational theory and economics."[10] His lifelong explorations led him not only to deep insights into human expertise and decision-making, but also to playing a pivotal role in shaping the early development of artificial intelligence (AI). Simon's groundbreaking work earned him the Nobel Prize in Economics in 1978, among other accolades.

Simon's extensive studies on expert professionals including doctors, scientists, and managers clearly demonstrated that intuition and expertise are founded on the ability to recognize patterns. In most instances these patterns are stored unconsciously. This creates a feeling of intuition, that something seems "right" even if it can't be explained consciously.

This means that to achieve expertise in our chosen area, we need to be consistently exposed to patterns so we can later recognize them. However, simply perceiving the patterns doesn't help much—we need to link them to outcomes.

Malcolm Gladwell's bestselling book *Outliers* proposed the "10,000-hour rule," suggesting that this period of practice was the foundation of excellence in any domain. This thesis was in fact based on a misinterpretation of research performed by "expert on expertise" Anders Ericsson, who later wrote that "unfortunately, this rule . . . is wrong in several ways."[11] Instead, he points to the development of the mental representation and pattern recognition that underpin excellence.

"The main thing that sets experts apart from the rest of us is that their years of practice have changed the neural circuitry in their brains to produce highly specialized mental representations, which in turn make possible the incredible memory, pattern recognition, problem-solving, and other sorts of advanced abilities needed to excel in their particular specialties," writes Ericsson in his book *Peak*.[12]

To recognize patterns in useful ways, linking them to outcomes and the most effective action, requires us to proactively develop useful patterns in our mind. Our primary task is, in fact, pattern formation.

We form these patterns as a distinctive, deeply personal lattice of connections in our minds. Our understanding of the world is based on how we bring together the fragments of the world we perceive to create meaning.

Our brains perceive patterns, recognize them as they recur, then expect them as similar conditions emerge. A tennis pro will anticipate when a familiar opponent is setting up a drop shot. A doctor will recognize patterns of symptoms to make a diagnosis. A market maker will notice indications of a secretive large buy order for a stock or commodity.

Pattern recognition is largely an unconscious process, but this is an enormous lost opportunity. We can accelerate and enhance the process by being conscious of the formation of patterns in our mind, considered in how elements mesh to form a whole, and deliberate in identifying patterns that may not be immediately apparent. This requires us to dig deep to reveal the essence of the domain we are studying. Often the most powerful way to do that is to create visual representations of knowledge that show the constituent concepts and the patterns that connect them.

The Power of Visual Thinking

Leonardo da Vinci is synonymous with genius. He is regarded not only as one of the greatest painters and sculptors in history, but also a scientist breaking new ground in fields as diverse as optics, human anatomy, and astronomy, as well as a prolific inventor, among other accomplishments. He was the archetypal Renaissance man.

Da Vinci's notebooks were his constant companions, capturing everything from his life, including his observations on nature, inventions, daily to-do lists, and far more. While he only completed 18 paintings that we know of (of course including the most famous painting in the world, the *Mona Lisa*), the thousands of pages of his notebooks that have survived until today include 13,000 sketches, including the famed *Vitruvian Man* that depicts ideal human proportions, shown in Figure 2.1. Not just da Vinci, but many of the most prodigious intellects through history, including Einstein, Tesla, Galileo, and Darwin, were deeply visual thinkers.

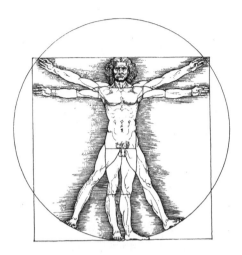

FIGURE 2.1   Leonardo da Vinci's *Vitruvian Man*

At the heart of the power of visualizing rather than using words is that you can transcend the sequential nature of writing. To develop expertise, we need to understand the manifold relationships between underlying concepts. Visual representations allow us to go beyond the linear to represent in one view the way many constituent ideas relate to form a whole. The phrase "I see" often means "I understand." When people say, "I see," they have literally created a visual representation in their mind.

> *We can accelerate the process of "seeing" by creating the visualizations that help us understand.*

It has been clearly demonstrated that the use of what is called spatial note-taking (in essence nonlinear notes such as maps and drawings) is strongly correlated with improved learning and comprehension.[13] The value of spatial notes depends on the skill of the individual in creating them, making visual note-taking an invaluable capability in our information-intensive environment.

The value, however, is not so much in taking notes when reading or in lectures or conversations. The real potential is having a central tool for capturing and continually refining your understanding of your domain of expertise. Visual frameworks are tools to support deep understanding of a domain and generate new insights.

Many visual tools have been developed to help us think effectively, build mental frameworks that help us understand, and map out conceptual landscapes. Some people have learned one of the numerous established techniques, while others create their own approaches.

A 2,000-fold increase in data over two decades has, not surprisingly, led to an explosion in the use of data and information visualization in business and news.[14] However, it is important to understand that information visualization and the visual concept frameworks that are the focus of this chapter are not the same thing. Well-designed information visualizations assist us by distilling and presenting data concisely and effectively. In contrast, visual concept frameworks are tools to develop knowledge and understanding. These can yield far greater value than simply helping us to digest quantitative information.

Framing Your Thinking

A vital difference between professional and amateur photographers is in how they frame their pictures. When they position their camera and click the shutter, they are choosing what will fit in the image. They select the borders, what the photograph encompasses, and what falls outside. In exactly the same way, when we seek to build expertise and understanding we have fundamental choices in how we frame our thinking.

What do you wish to understand? In what specific domain have you chosen to develop world-class expertise? What is the focus of your interest and attention? What are the topics on which you want to know the latest?

In selecting your frame, the most important consideration is utility. Some topics can simply be too broad to pretend to keep up with. Being more focused allows you to maintain your edge and expertise. Leading venture capitalist Gary Swart selects the companies he pays attention to by a number of parameters, including how well they fit with his established areas of expertise.[15]

Most of us aren't attempting to create frameworks that describe life, the universe, and everything. While some have valiantly tried, it is hardly helpful to embark on that journey if your objective is to tame overwhelm. Selecting a frame is liberating. It means we are no longer trying to boil the ocean. It lets us see what should and should not be included.

A startup founder might develop a framework for the state and evolution of the industry sector that she is targeting. She may also choose to frame developments in new funding structures if she thinks she might go beyond traditional angel or venture capital investment to build her company.

A corporate leader may want to consider the implications of rapid shifts in the nature of work. This is of course a huge topic. It will usually be more useful to select more specific frames, such as capturing the core ideas of hybrid work, clarifying important concepts such as scalable learning, or understanding the dynamics of how to attract and retain talented employees.

Start by naming your framework with a few words that give clarity on the topic and what is included and excluded. This is the seed around which you will organize your ideas. When preparing my keynote speeches, which I build as frameworks, my first step is to agree on a working title with my client, so we have a common guiding concept.

There are three primary structures for building concept frameworks: trees, networks, and systems, as shown in Figure 2.2. Not surprisingly, each of these reflects the natural world. As in nature, these architectures of thought are not distinct but are connected and overlap. Let us explore these structures in turn and how we can best use them. We each have our own cognitive style. As you read about the techniques, consider which approaches best suit how you think.

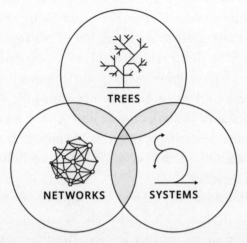

FIGURE 2.2   Three Ways of Representing Knowledge

Trees

We are told that at the center of the beautiful and bountiful Garden of Eden stood the tree of knowledge. Adam and Eve, the first man and woman, were instructed to tend the garden. They were told they could partake of the fruit of almost any tree in the garden but were sternly forbidden to eat from the tree of knowledge. To cut to the chase, they did, and for their sin were banished from the garden forever, their eyes having been opened to the world.

The tree of knowledge is a powerful metaphor: understanding can be very usefully represented as a tree, with its trunk, roots, branches, foliage, and fruit elucidating how concepts are related.

The structure of successive divisions from the tree trunk to branches, then twigs and leaves is evident across natural life, including the plant kingdom and multiple aspects of our underlying biology. In a similar way, our thinking often follows hierarchical structures, dividing central concepts into components and in turn subsidiary ideas.

Trees, like many other natural phenomena, have a fractal structure, in which the morphology of how branches and twigs divide is the same at all levels. When Hollywood movies use computer-generated imagery (CGI) to generate natural scenes, the trees are formed using fractal algorithms.

Third-century Greek philosopher Porphyry presented Aristotelian categories as a series of divisions, which inspired others to later create what were called Porphyrian trees, representing the system of relationships between concepts in arboreal form, seen in Figure 2.3.

FIGURE 2.3 A Porphyrian Tree Representing the Organization of the Sciences

The analogy remains powerful and valuable in how we build understanding. Elon Musk, responding to a question on how he is able to learn so much, advised that "it is important to view knowledge as sort of a semantic tree—make sure you understand the fundamental principles, i.e., the trunk and big branches, before you get into the leaves/details or there is nothing for them to hang on to."[16]

The contours of these "semantic trees" are shaped by the process of building knowledge. As we consider the many forks that generate our trees of knowledge, we need to learn how to navigate between the different levels, from the primary ideas through to the minutiae.

Logical Levels

In the storied history of Harvard Business School since its establishment in 1908, the 1963 MBA intake was different. For the first time ever, women were admitted, with among the 8 ambitious women accepted to the 600-strong cohort a young woman named Barbara Minto.[17] She had applied out of concern for her job security as a secretary in a railway company, and despite her lack of an undergraduate degree, aced the entrance examination and was accepted.

On her graduation Minto became the first professional female hire of preeminent management consultancy McKinsey & Co., soon finding her place teaching its consultants to think logically. As she traveled between offices in the United States and Europe running workshops on how to write well-structured client reports, she developed an approach that she called the Pyramid Principle. This approach remains deeply embedded in McKinsey's culture and has been adopted by many other major consulting firms.

The essence of the Pyramid Principle is identifying hierarchies in thinking, from the organizing concept at the pinnacle to the underlying ideas, and in turn to the subsidiary concepts, through to the base of the pyramid, as illustrated in Figure 2.4.

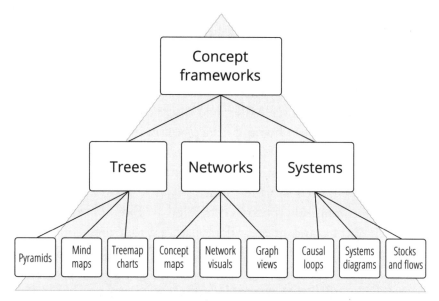

FIGURE 2.4 Organizing Concepts in a Pyramid Structure

The core of Minto's principle can be explained by two of her rules: "Ideas at any level in the pyramid must always be summaries of the ideas grouped below them," and "Ideas in each grouping must always be the same kind of idea."[18]

The pyramid diagram of course looks just like an organizational chart, with the CEO at the top and their direct reports in turn below them, depicting a hierarchy. So why do I propose that we talk about "logical levels" rather than hierarchies?

The word "hierarchy" comes from the Greek *hierarkhes*, meaning "holy ruler." It implies that there is an ultimate apex. However, unless our framework encompasses the entire universe, it limits our thinking to consider there is a pinnacle that we do not think beyond. Rather, we need to be thinking in terms of moving up and down logical levels, sometimes higher or lower than our original concept or framework. Hierarchies are inherently limited. Thinking in logical levels liberates us to move between levels of abstraction or concreteness to match our intent.

To do this we need to think in terms of "chunks" of information. The term "chunking" comes from one of the most cited papers in psychology, "The Magic Number Seven, Plus or Minus Two: Some Limits on Our Capacity for Processing Information."[19] Harvard psychologist George Miller had discovered that people could usually retain between five and nine pieces of information simultaneously. However, if they "chunked" this collection of information into recognizable units, they could in turn save around seven of these chunks in their short-term memory.

This was famously illustrated by Herbert Simon's experiments in which chess grand masters demonstrated that they could with a brief glance memorize all the positions of a chess game in play. There are a limited number of common arrangements of the pieces across the board that they could readily commit to memory. Inexperienced players failed completely at this task, as without those organizing chunks of the chessboard in their mind, they had to try to individually remember the position of each piece. If the pieces did not show an actual chess game in progress but were laid out randomly, the grandmasters performed no better than amateurs, since they could not draw on the patterns they had memorized.[20]

The facility to move between logical levels is one of the simplest and most powerful conceptual tools we have. Two simple questions help us to shift between logical levels in our thinking:

To move up:
What is this an example or instance of?

To move down:
What is an example or instance of this?

To illustrate this, consider a car. To find a higher logical level, you ask what cars are an example of. There are many possible answers, including road transportation, inventions, or status symbols. All are valid, but each provides a very different frame for thinking about cars.

To move to a lower logical level, you identify examples or instances of cars. Again, you have a choice: you could list car styles, such as convertibles, sedans, station wagons, and four-wheel drives, or car brands like General Motors, Volkswagen, and Tesla, or car components such as chassis, wheels, tires, dashboards, and hand brakes. Deftly shifting between logical levels in your thinking can be a highly creative process, generating new conceptual structures and manifesting new possibilities. Sometimes, however, the relationships are more nuanced.

Thinking Meta

As a youth over a summer, I read the first edition of Douglas Hofstadter's *Gödel, Escher, Bach*, one mind-bending section of a chapter a day. It remains one of the most influential books in my life. The book weaves together an extraordinary tapestry of ideas to point to the nature of consciousness and consider whether machines could become conscious. At the center of its argument and the very structure of the book was the concept of "strange loops," illustrated by Johann Sebastian Bach's endlessly rising melodies, M.C. Escher's impossible recursive drawings, and mathematician Kurt Gödel's tectonic Incompleteness Theorem, which proved that no internally consistent system of thinking can be complete.[21]

Hofstadter's masterpiece was written when he was still a junior academic, having barely finished his PhD. It launched him immediately onto the global stage, with the book receiving accolades and awards including the Pulitzer Prize for nonfiction. One of the reviews was by writer Martin Gardner, who wrote about the book that, "every few decades, an unknown author brings out a book of such depth, clarity, range, wit, beauty and originality that it is recognized at once as a major literary event."[22]

At the time Gardner was in his third decade of writing what was probably the most popular column in *Scientific American* magazine, "Mathematical Games," which delved into the delights of "recreational mathematics." Shortly after Hofstadter accepted the daunting task of becoming Gardner's successor, renaming the column "Metamagical Themas," an anagram of the preceding feature.

The *meta* Hofstadter used to coin the word *metamagical* was originally a prefix meaning "above" or "beyond," as for example in *metaphysics*, but it has now become a word in its own right, popularized by Hofstadter and particularly cherished by the software development community.

Historically *meta* meant moving to a higher logical level, as is required in almost all software architectures. Now it is often used with the more precise meaning of recursion, meaning something being about itself, for example data about data, jokes about jokes, thinking about thinking, or movies about movies (most obviously films such as *Adaptation*, *The Player*, or Fellini's *8½*, but self-reference is becoming endemic in entertainment; think *Being John Malkovich*, *Deadpool*, or elements of almost any of the more recent crop of comic-inspired films). While the word has unfortunately been commandeered by the-company-formerly-known-as-Facebook, it is a valuable concept and should continue to be used in its own right.

Evolving information flows, the foundational role of software in our lives, and shifting thinking paradigms are leading to an increasingly recursive world. "Thinking meta" is often a highly relevant tool, developing our facility at perceiving loops, seeing systems, and assigning meaningful structure to new thoughts and ideas.

Mind Maps

The most commonly used visual framework based on hierarchical structures is the mind map. Tony Buzan first shared his idea of a visual representation of ideas in his 1970s BBC Radio program *Use Your Head*. He went on to reach a far larger audience in 1996 with *The Mind Map Book*, later claiming that 250 million people worldwide use his techniques. The technique is commonly taught in schools, and a profusion of software tools are available to help us create mind maps.

The prominent innovation in Buzan's visuals was the idea of what he called "radial thinking," placing the principal concept in the center of the diagram rather than at the bottom or side of the page.[23] Mind maps are in essence hierarchies. However, reconfiguration of placing the concept in the middle aligns better with how we represent knowledge in our mind. There are four primary principles in creating mind maps:

1. **Organizing concept at the center.** All mind maps place the core idea in the middle of the diagram, with subsidiary ideas radiating out from the center.

2. **Hierarchical structure.** Subsidiary concepts stem from the seed concept, often with the thickness of lines reducing as they fork to lower-level ideas.

3. **Visual elements.** Buzan recommended using images wherever possible to illustrate and evoke ideas, particularly for the central concept, and to use different colors for the lines and nodes.

4. **Associations.** Where there are connections between elements, especially across different forks in the map, draw lines between them.

For example, an executive may be considering how best to shift to hybrid work, in which employees share their working time among office, home, or other locations. He might choose to create a mind map of the main ideas to clarify his thinking and surface other issues that he should take into account. Figure 2.5 presents a highly simplified mind map of concepts surrounding hybrid work. This kind of diagram could provide an initial frame to discuss and develop appropriate strategies and work policies.

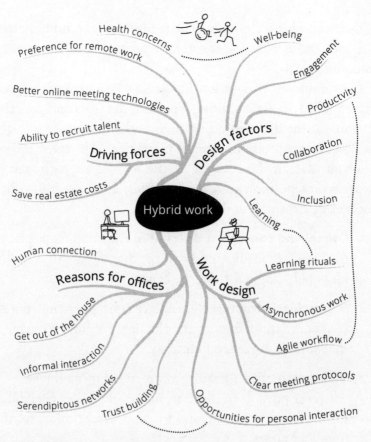

FIGURE 2.5 Mind Map of Key Concepts in Hybrid Work

Networks

The relatively recent advent of network science has shown us that networks are at the center of not just technology, infrastructure, and society, but also many facets of biology.[24] Our brains, too, are best understood as networks. Massive funding has gone into the study of neurological networks as a compelling route to understand the essential nature of our minds.[25]

Our cognition is based on associations between experiences and ideas. The well-known catchphrase "neurons that fire together, wire together," neatly captures our longstanding understanding of how our neural networks are formed.[26] Simply put, we build associations through experience.

This process, continued throughout our lives, generates what cognitive psychologists call the "semantic networks" that link meaning in our ideas, thoughts, and perceptions. These are the foundation of how we think and understand the world.

No doubt you've experienced suddenly wondering why you are thinking about something that seems very random. If your memory serves you well, you can track back the sequence of steps between your thoughts from what may have been a very different starting point. The leaps of thought you took are unique to you, reflecting the associations you have built up over many years. Capturing and deliberately building the networks of ideas in our mind is an exceptionally valuable approach to developing our knowledge.

Perceiving Categories

The title of renowned linguist George Lakoff's seminal book *Women, Fire, and Dangerous Things: What Categories Reveal About the Mind* was inspired by the Australian indigenous language Dyirbal, in which these concepts are all of the same type. As the subtitle suggests, Lakoff strongly argues that the categories we use reflect our cognitive structures, not any objective reality.[27] In fact, categories are integral to how we conceive of the world.

The explosion of information over the past decades has forced us to reexamine how we categorize information and ideas. Not so long ago librarians would apply their despotic power to select where in the Dewey system (and thus on the shelves) a book could be found. Scientists of all persuasions created taxonomies to allocate new ideas as they saw fit. Yet in a connected world people suddenly found they had the power to allocate their own categories to ideas. All they had to do was create a tag.

Thus "folksonomies" were born, in which common folk together started to create new categories and connections with the simple act of tagging content in ways they found meaningful. We are now in a world in which "everything is miscellaneous," in the words of author David Weinberger, sorted into a plethora of different categories, depending on people's perceptions.[28]

Adding tags to content is one of the easiest and most effective ways to surface the connections that form concept networks. As you work to build personal knowledge from pervasive information, a primary task is choosing the categories for everything interesting you find. Simply tagging content with meaningful labels as you encounter it in fact generates knowledge by creating meaningful patterns and revealing relationships between ideas.

Concept networks can be represented in a variety of ways. Most connected note-taking software, which we will look at later in this chapter, has the ability to display "graph views" showing the connections you have made between your notes. Classic network visualizations, often used to map social connections, can also be applied to ideas. Another useful tool to capture networked thinking was first used to study how people learn.

Concept Maps

As a professor of education at Cornell University, Joseph Novak researched how science students developed understanding of their subjects. He developed what he called "concept maps" to represent how they formed their knowledge, subsequently using the maps created to help others learn the same topics.

The essence of concept maps is portraying the relationships between ideas. The elements that underlie concepts are linked by verbs describing the relationship between them. This gives full latitude to express all kinds of relationship, including causality, logical levels, or any of a variety of abstract or concrete connections.

A concept map is used to clarify and communicate understanding. Fittingly, Tim Berners-Lee's original proposal for the World Wide Web opened with a concept map laying out the network of relationships between the ideas in his submission.[29]

For example, a business leader may be intrigued by the idea of "scalable learning" proposed by prominent business thinker John Hagel. Hagel suggests that the rise of exponential digital technologies means institutions must shift from the "scalable efficiency" that characterized large business in the last century to the "scalable learning" they require to succeed today.[30] To grasp the concept and share it with colleagues the executive may create a simple concept map such as the one shown in Figure 2.6, depicting the relationship between the underlying ideas.

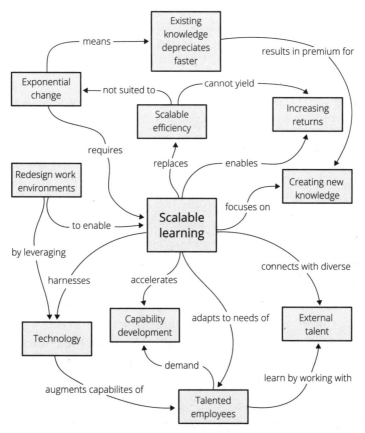

FIGURE 2.6   A Simple Concept Map
Describing the Idea of Scalable Learning

Trees and networks are both valuable approaches to connect and represent our knowledge. However, sometimes the world is considerably more complex than can be described with these structures. We need to learn to think in terms of systems.

Systems

Jay Forrester grew up on a ranch in rural Nebraska, becoming attuned not only to the dynamics of the weather, crops, and livestock, but also the complexity of farming economics. Reflecting on how his upbringing shaped his life's journey, he noted that "supply and demand, changing prices and costs, and economic pressures of agriculture become a very personal, powerful, and dominating part of life."[31] He began to notice patterns in the apparently unpredictable fluctuations of farms' fortunes.

After graduating from University of Nebraska at the outset of World War II, Forrester moved to MIT in Boston for his graduate studies. The lab in which he worked designed feedback control systems for rotating guns and radar antennas to improve positioning accuracy. When he became a faculty member at what would later become the MIT Sloan School of Management, General Electric executives invited him to help them manage inordinate production fluctuations in one of their household appliance plants in Kentucky. Forrester noticed that the patterns that created these swings could be understood using the same feedback loops as the guiding systems he had helped build.

Forrester went on to create the field of "systems dynamics," which studies how systems as a whole function. When in the late 1990s I went on a pilgrimage to MIT's Systems Dynamics Group to discuss the application of systems modeling to intellectual capital in financial markets, I was in awe as I wandered through the corridors of the birthplace of modern systems thinking.

Forrester's simple yet powerful insight is that the world is not linear. Things feed on themselves. A little enthusiasm that generates results can spark greater excitement. A price leap in a stock or cryptocurrency can attract more buyers and further surges. The complexity of the world transcends simple relationships, and as we build our frameworks to elucidate ideas, we need to consider the loops as well as lines of influence. We need to understand and look for the two kinds of feedback loops: reinforcing and balancing.

Reinforcing Feedback Loops

It took wunderkind complexity scientist W. Brian Arthur to point out in the late 1980s what is now patently obvious: in some markets (most obviously but not only technology platforms) success breeds success. Instagram was an instant hit at its launch in late 2010, reaching 10 million users within 13 months from launch. Seven months later it hit 50 million users, just after it was acquired by Facebook for $1 billion. It now has over 1 billion users.[32]

Amazon sported red ink at the bottom of its financial results for each of its first 10 years after it was founded, leading to widespread investor skepticism as to whether its business model would ever be profitable. Jeff Bezos was clear on what he was trying to build: a model in which improved performance would feed on itself. In 2000 he drew his conception of the company's business model on a napkin, as shown in Figure 2.7.[33] The positive feedback loop he envisaged has continued to grow. Amazon surpassed $1 trillion in market capitalization in January 2020.

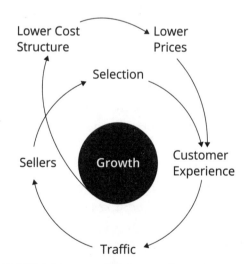

FIGURE 2.7 The Reinforcing Feedback Loops Underlying Amazon's Business Model

Reinforcing feedback loops do not always lead to greater wealth or happy outcomes. When companies lose staff, the workload of the remaining employees increases, leading to stress, declining morale, and further resignations. On a macro scale, as the planet warms, higher temperatures are feeding on themselves through a variety of mechanisms, including melting polar ice releasing methane and reducing the surface area reflecting the sun's rays, accelerating the pace that ice cover decreases.

Also, not all feedback loops amplify outcomes. Some balance and thus reduce change.

Balancing Feedback Loops

Balancing feedback loops work to stabilize the system. All life demonstrates marvelous balancing mechanisms; otherwise, anything that pushed an organism off kilter would kill it. A simple example is human body temperature. When we get too warm, we sweat, with the drying of our perspiration in any breeze cooling us, while our inbuilt response of shivering in the cold warms us.

There are ample illustrations in business of balancing feedback loops. Anyone who has gone through a change management process in a large organization will have seen firsthand some of the wide array of human responses that countervail management efforts. These "corporate antibodies" are striving to return the organization to its prior state. The many efforts over the years to reform the deep dysfunctions of the US healthcare system consistently encounter balancing feedback that supports the maintenance of the status quo.

Systems Diagrams

Systems diagrams can be immensely valuable tools for seeking to understand in depth any complex system—natural, societal, or organizational. These visualizations endeavor to capture the essential interlocking reinforcing and balancing feedback loops that make up a system. By their nature they necessarily take you beyond linear thinking to a richer representation of the real world.

An organizational leader may want to think through the dynamics of attracting and retaining talent, including where the company may be able to engineer reinforcing feedback loops with positive outcomes, as well as potential risk factors. A highly simplified systems diagram summarizing how a leader might think about these relationships is shown in Figure 2.8. In the diagram an arrow with a plus sign (+) indicates a reinforcing relationship increasing the linked element, while an arrow with a minus sign (–) shows a balancing relationship of reduction. In some cases, a positive feedback loop is created, but also with dampening factors.

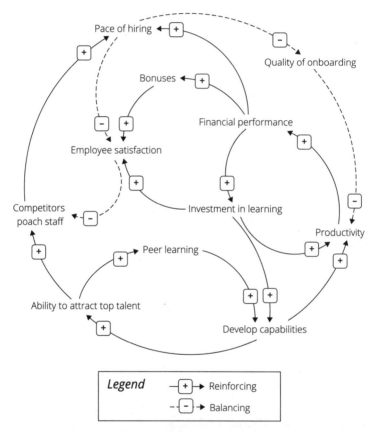

FIGURE 2.8 Simple Systems Diagram of Attracting and Retaining Talent

Designing systems diagrams is often a subtle process that requires deep thinking. To learn in more detail how to apply systems thinking, including the different systems diagram styles such as causal loops and stocks and flows, refer to the Resources section at the end of this book.

Even if you don't choose to represent systems visually, it is always valuable to look for reinforcing and balancing feedback loops around you. If you perceive a possible feedback loop, make a note and see if you can place it in the concept frameworks you are building. This single step can substantially enhance your understanding of the principles underlying your area of expertise. Sensitivity to seeing feedback and recursion is a vital capability in a complex world.

Many of the frameworks that enable better thinking are visual in nature. However, other valuable approaches to capturing connections between ideas include index cards, software, and writing.

Connected Notes

There is a solid case that the fulcrum of human history was the invention of writing, enabling us to capture our knowledge, pass on stories and lessons to other generations, and transcend the inherent fallibility of our memories. Our cognition is deeply limited; writing allows us to develop and structure our thinking, as well as recall what we have thought in the past. Yet writing is inherently sequential, while the world is not.

Linear notes, simply writing ideas or references as you find them, are valuable in being able to come back to them and later use them in refinding sources or building more structured ideas. These can be on paper, in digital form, or in the margins of books.

As entrepreneur Richard Branson says, if you don't take notes, you won't have access to the most useful ideas you devise or encounter. "I go through dozens of notebooks every year and write down everything that occurs to me each day. Some of the ideas contained inside end up turning into reality, and some don't—but they are all noteworthy," he says. "An idea not written down is an idea lost. It doesn't matter how you record your notes—as long as you do."[34]

Taking notes of any kind is an invaluable starting point for developing your thinking. Once you have captured an idea, you can far more readily connect it to any existing or new concepts that come to mind.

Connected notes go beyond sequential writing to capture some of the multitude of possible relationships between ideas, beginning to emulate the underlying structure of how we think. Useful concept frameworks don't need to be explicitly visual. Any system that helps you capture or make explicit the connections between ideas can be enormously valuable.

Interconnected Index Cards

As a devastated Germany exited World War II, 18-year-old Niklas Luhmann chose to study law, believing that it could help avoid the traumatic social breakdown he had experienced through his youth. After becoming a lawyer and then deciding he disliked having to work for clients, he entered public service and started studying sociology in his own time, successfully applying for a scholarship to Harvard to learn more about social systems. On his return to Germany at age 35 he commenced his academic career, finally earning his PhD at 39.[35] He became not only a highly influential sociologist and systems theorist, but also one of the most prolific, writing more than 70 books and almost 400 academic publications. Each year of the last three decades of his life he published on average more than two books and 13 often-extensive publications. Luhmann credited his phenomenal productivity to the use of his note-taking system, which he called *Zettelkasten*, meaning "slip box."

The "slips" were what we call index cards, each numbered and placed in a series of boxes. Luhmann developed a complex system of cross-referencing the cards through tags and hierarchies, through his life amassing a richly interlinked collection of 90,000 cards.

Luhmann was not the first to write ideas and concepts on index cards and form links between them. Influential scientists and thinkers who used very similar systems before him include the great mathematician and philosopher Gottfried Leibniz and Carl Linnaeus, who created our modern biological taxonomic system.

Linnaeus's life was dedicated to using structure to make sense of excessive information. It was only toward the end of his life that he started using index cards, having used lists earlier in his career, then progressing to depicting hierarchical structures on a page. Science historians observed that, "as his work progressed and the volume of data increased, Linnaeus found himself overwhelmed by new information. He had to move on from simple tables and diagrams to more complex and flexible ways of organizing his data."[36] He found the solution in his compilation of richly indexed cards.

Software Tools for Connected Notes

I remember the fun I had when Apple introduced its HyperCard software in 1987, which enabled hyperlinks between what were effectively digital index cards, years before the World Wide Web was created and undoubtedly inspiring the structure of the web in its early years. Luhmann and his peers had linked their physical cards through complex numbering and tagging. Now anyone could for the first time create their own digital "hyperlinks" between text and ideas.

Bill Atkinson, an engineer at Apple, had come up with the idea after taking LSD. "Poets, artists, musicians, physicists, chemists, biologists, mathematicians, and economists all have separate pools of knowledge, but are hindered from sharing and finding the deeper connections. . . . I thought if we could encourage sharing of ideas between different areas of knowledge, perhaps more of the bigger picture would emerge, and eventually more wisdom might develop. Sort of a trickle-up theory of information leading to knowledge leading to wisdom. This was the underlying inspiration for HyperCard."[37]

At the opening of this chapter, you learned about TheBrain, which Jerry Michalski uses to store and connect his information and ideas. Today there are a wealth of tools to take networked notes, including a number of new offerings, suggesting the demand for these kinds of tools is increasing in our information-saturated world.

Many simple note-taking tools, such as Evernote and Notion, can include links between notes, helping users to build connections between ideas, though they are not ideally suited to the task. Some people hijack productivity software such as Trello to segment and link concepts or collections of lists.

Connected note-taking software is a rapidly growing sector, seemingly having hit the zeitgeist over the past couple of years. Roam Research was built as a prototype in 2017, growing rapidly and attracting enthusiastic proselytizers, giving rise to the term "roamcult." Eminent venture capitalist Brad Feld reports, "I use a lot of different software. Nothing has had as much impact on me . . . as Roam."[38] Other players include open-source alternative Obsidian, which I use, which boasts its own devoted user community. For anyone who is drawn to investing time and effort into connecting their thinking, these can be invaluable tools.

Framing by Communicating

Iconoclastic scientist Richard Feynman, voted by his peers one of the greatest physicists of all time, was passionate about the power and impact of good teaching, not just for students, but also for the educator. "If you want to master something, teach it," he reputedly said. "The more you teach, the more you learn."

You discover whether you truly understand something when you try to explain it to others.

One of the best prompts to clarify your comprehension of a field is to create a syllabus (which is in fact a framework) and help one or more students to develop their own understanding. Good teachers of course do not spout a litany of facts; they help their students to make sense of what's important, how elements relate, and the structures that underlie clear mental models for the topic. Learning in the expectation of having to teach others has been proven to improve how students organize their knowledge.[39] This so-called protégé effect has been clearly demonstrated by the superior learning performance of those students who are also tutoring.

I find that some of the smartest people find it difficult to explicate their thinking. They have highly refined mental frameworks that underpin their understanding, but the structures often lie largely below their conscious minds. They only distill their syntheses when they are forced to, when they have to for their work or choose to deliver a speech or write an article or book.

Warren Buffett uses writing to test and refine his thinking. "I learn while I think when I write it out," he says. "Some of the things I think I think, I find don't make any sense when I start trying to write them down and explain them to people. . . . And if it can't stand applying pencil to paper, you'd better think it through some more."[40]

Paul Graham, cofounder of the world's largest accelerator, Y Combinator, writes regular essays on whatever he's thinking about at the time. "*Essayer* is the French verb meaning 'to try' and an *essai* is an attempt. An essay is something you write to try to figure something out," he writes. "Just as inviting people over forces you to clean up your apartment, writing something that other people will read forces you to think well."[41]

If you are giving a presentation on your field of expertise or writing a piece about a specific aspect of it, you need to structure the flow of your ideas so that your audience will grasp key messages and be left with new understanding. Communicating well requires pulling back to consider what is important, how concepts relate, what metaphors are useful, and the most logical sequence of ideas. Jeff Bezos forced his managers to summarize their thoughts in memos of no more than six pages, noting, "There is no way to write a six-page, narratively structured memo and not have clear thinking."[42]

As you might guess, I don't entirely agree with this. I have read memos and articles that demonstrate highly confused thinking. The discipline of structured writing is immensely beneficial but is not a sure remedy. On the other hand, it is nigh impossible to create a visual representation of your thinking that doesn't clarify your reasoning for yourself and others.

The most effective way to distill your thoughts is to write an account that includes a visual summary of your logic.

The reality is that most of the framing I do is driven by my client work, researching and thinking deeply to develop a keynote or the structure for a strategy session. I work for a defined outcome and audience. It is the same for most of the people I know; they distill their insights so they can write a blog post or make a presentation. The synthesis happens in the process of communicating or teaching what they know, and in so doing they identify the gaps they need to fill to build a truly comprehensive frame and understanding.

Framing the Future

Every decision you make is about the future. You can't change the past, however hard you try. The only thing you can change, where your decisions and actions can have an impact, is the future. Yet how can we make sense of the extraordinary uncertainty of the future?

I often say that "everyone needs to be their own futurist." You can't outsource your thinking about the future. While the practice of the art and science of foresight is beyond the ambit of this book, the fundamental mindset and many of the tools used are reflected through this book.

Whether you are considering an area of expertise or seeking to make better decisions in your business or life, explicitly thinking about the future can be very helpful. Future-oriented frameworks are marvelous tools to sensitize you to the most interesting, relevant information that could impact your decisions and actions.

Making Predictions for Sense-Making

We all know that it is difficult to make predictions, especially about the future.[43] Yet in building frameworks that are useful to us, it is perfectly valid to make educated guesses on when possible future events might happen. If our frameworks are in the first instance primarily for ourselves, taking a stab at predictions is in fact a wonderful tool for filtering information. It prompts us to look for and assess inputs that either support our estimates or help us adjust them. In this case the primary purpose of our prediction is not to be right, but to help us look for the information that will suggest that our prediction is too early, too late, or just about right.

A very useful way to represent possible future technologies and developments is by creating visual timelines. They may show when events might occur on a time scale from left to right, or sometimes as concentric circles rippling out from the present. These structures align with the way we mentally represent time, helping us make sense of the forecasts.[44]

My most widely seen work is probably the Newspaper Extinction Timeline my firm Future Exploration Network created in 2010. This visual framework depicted years for when news-on-paper would be become "insignificant" for every country in the world. It was very widely shared, appearing in major newspapers (ahem) and online publications in over 30 countries in the first week after publication, being seen by many millions of readers.[45] References to the timeline still regularly appear in the global media.

It is safe to say that the framework was highly contentious, and some of my forecasts proved to be badly wrong, in particular the lead forecasts of 2017 for the United States and 2019 for the United Kingdom, though many of the forecasts for the coming decade are looking likely to be fairly accurate. The point is, I didn't create the timeline to be right. I have long publicly said I don't believe in making predictions, because they will almost always be wrong.[46] In this case, I stated at the outset that I offered specific predictions to make people think more about the forces shifting news delivery from paper to new channels, noting that it was intended to "stimulate useful strategic conversations." It certainly achieved its desired impact, being frequently discussed in board meetings and publicly referenced by many business and government leaders.[47] One of the world's largest media conglomerates was prompted to build its own internal models to estimate when its newspapers would cease printing.[48]

When you put a stake in the ground for the occurrence, timing, or probability of a possible future event, it immediately puts any new information into perspective. In the case of a predicted timeline for a new technology to come to market or be widely adopted, relevant news items can be used to reassess the original time frame. If the prediction is the likelihood of the election of a political candidate, for example, any news can be assessed as to whether it might increase or decrease that probability.

Scenarios Surface Signals

The US Defense Logistics Agency (DLA) employs 26,000 staff who manage the supply of $40 billion in goods and services to the US military across 28 countries. To manage the extreme uncertainty of change across its operations, the agency undertook a scenario planning initiative, in which teams define a small set of possible future worlds relevant to critical decisions.[49] One of the primary applications of the scenarios was to sensitize the DLA's staff and executives to eventualities that could impact its ability to achieve its objectives. In addition to providing a strategic framework for the organization's planning, the scenarios helped identify "weak signals," seemingly minor developments that could lead to dramatic and significant shifts.

A richly developed set of scenarios is far more valuable than a simple prediction. Useful scenarios provide not just an evocative picture of each future, but also a plausible and detailed narrative of the sequence of events that leads there. Our minds grasp stories and mental pictures far better than abstract ideas or concepts. Having a small set of future worlds helps us interpret almost any new information by seeing where it fits among the scenarios' narratives. If it doesn't fit anywhere, then it can be even more useful by prompting revision of the underlying thinking.

Unfortunately, few companies have the appetite for this protracted process, yet in the many scenario projects I have run I have consistently seen immense value created, especially through aligning executives' mental models and supporting more sophisticated decision-making. Individuals who wish to readily benefit from scenario thinking can draw on the many solid sets of scenarios published by major consulting firms, international agencies such as the OECD and World Economic Forum, government bodies including the CIA and the European Union, and companies like Shell. Spending time with one (or more) of the public scenario reports that seems relevant to your work will give you valuable perspectives for filtering new information.

Creating Your Own Visual Frameworks

When, as has frequently happened over the years, I am asked how I keep on top of accelerating change, sometimes my joking response has been to suggest they read my book *Thriving on Overload* when I get around to writing it (which I am extremely glad to have finally done!). If pressed to offer just one tip at the heart of my capabilities, I recommended developing their own visual frameworks to help make sense of change.

I have publicly shared many of the frameworks I have created on a wide range of topics, such as the future of media, the transformation of business and government, enterprise technology, industry disruption, and the role of artificial intelligence, as well as worked extensively with corporate clients to help them design frameworks for their internal sense-making.[50]

To illustrate the high-level process I use for creating the visual frameworks, consider the very widely shared *Humans in the Future of Work* framework I created in 2016, seen in Figure 2.9.[51] I would probably adjust a couple of things today if I came back to it, but the basic concepts remain just as relevant.

The process is slightly different if you are creating a framework for communicating to others rather than just yourself, but the essence is the same. Either way you will get immense value from the rigor of explicitly framing your thinking.

1. Select Scope

A framework requires a clear scope, best generated with a descriptive title that will make sense to others as well as you. In this case the intent was clear, to describe the role of humans in work in a changing world. In other situations, you may need to be precise in selecting your organizing concept. Should your framework really aim to cover developments in energy? Or perhaps it would be more useful with a more specific frame, such as the state of household energy provision in the United States (if you work at an American electric utility, for example)?

2. Consider the Central Logic

What is the narrative or logic at the center of your framework? In *Humans in the Future of Work*, there is a logic that flows from left to right, from what is disrupting work, to the emerging role of humans, and on to the implications for organizations. Other frameworks I have created are structured from underlying foundations from the bottom up through layers of higher-order implications. Some are circular, with core concepts in the middle and interrelated elements around them. Before deciding the final visual layout, consider the fundamental ideas, which concepts support others, and whether there are complex relationships to portray such as causality or interdependence. If there is no particular logic

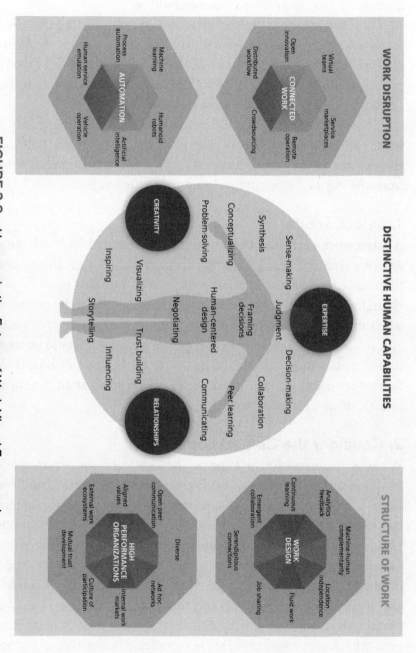

FIGURE 2.9 Humans in the Future of Work Visual Framework

or underlying structure, perhaps a mind map or other similar visual will be sufficient.

3. Brainstorm Concepts

To build a comprehensive framework, make a list of all possible relevant elements. Start organizing them into categories if these are evident. This can be done in a mind map, but it can work simply to make lists of relevant concepts in a document. The idea is to scan widely for what might fit in the framework. Exhaust your own imagination and then peruse ideas from those who are looking at similar spaces. If possible, get other people's input or even run formal brainstorming sessions.

4. Rearrange Elements

You now need to take the universe of concepts you have generated to a structure that makes sense. What are the core ideas within the scope you have selected? Identifying these can be harder than it appears. You need to play with different ideas and wording to identify the right organizing concepts, sometimes restructuring and rearranging extensively until a logical structure starts to emerge. What fits where, and why? You may need to combine similar ideas, or you might realize that a concept has more than one aspect and needs to be divided into parts. For *Humans in the Future of Work* I had to consolidate the many distinctive human capabilities into a limited number that made sense, eventually landing on the categories of Expertise, Creativity, and Relationships.

5. Elucidate Relationships

It is time to consider in more depth the relationships within your framework. Does your original idea for the central logic or narrative still hold? What is the connection between your core concepts? Are the lower-level elements just instances of the higher-order concepts? Or do they have a different kind of relationship? In *Humans in the Future of Work* I laid out the various human capabilities between Expertise, Creativity, and Relationships, considering where each fit relative to the organizing concepts. As I grappled with creating my Future of Media Strategic Framework in 2006, which was subsequently viewed over a million times, I ended up putting a yin-yang symbol at the center, with Consumer and Creator as the two elementary intertwined facets of the emerging media landscape.[52]

6. Develop the Visual Framework

I usually sketch my ideas on paper first to work out possible configurations and layouts, then use simple software to see how they look on a page. I am not a designer, but I work closely with designers to take my concepts to a visually attractive layout. While many designers can take a well-defined concept and make it look good, try to find sophisticated designers who can suggest different layouts and visual logics to best articulate your thinking.

Implementing the Power of Framing

Framing is a vital tool to build understanding and expertise. It also provides the foundation for the synthesis that supports powerful insight and better decisions, which we will examine in detail in Chapter 5.

As you develop your powers for thriving, you need to select the approaches you will use to frame your thinking and expertise development. We all think differently; we need to discover for ourselves the kinds of frameworks we find most useful, whether you use one of the methods covered in this chapter or your own approach.

The power of filtering covered in the next chapter builds on and applies the concept frameworks you have created, using them to help distinguish the signals that are relevant to your purpose from the noise you can ignore.

EXERCISES

Framework Topics

Choose titles for your first visual framework(s), on an area of expertise you are actively developing. The titles should clearly define the scope.

Initial Framing

Build a draft visualization of a selected area of expertise, using any technique you choose. The important thing is to start. Come back to it repeatedly to refine it, and try more than one approach.

Framework Styles

Having experimented, which approaches to framing or note-taking (from those described in this chapter or others you may have come across or created) might you adopt? Which others do you intend to try?

Framing Tools and Practices

What other practices might you implement to enhance your capabilities at framing (e.g., taking notes, adding structure to your notes, using connected note-taking software, tagging your notes, writing, teaching, creating technology timelines, scenario planning, other)?

CHAPTER 3

THE POWER OF FILTERING

Discern What Serves You

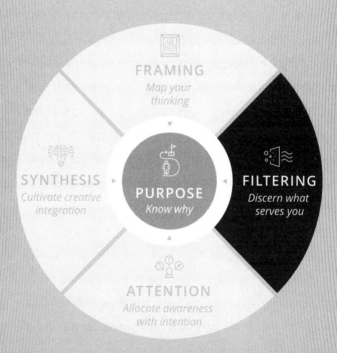

Some ideas are better than others. The machinery for distinguishing them is an essential tool in dealing with the world and especially in dealing with the future.[1]

—Carl Sagan, astronomer and cocreator, *Cosmos*

Our brains are wired to constantly seek new information. We need to develop our faculties of discernment, recognizing what matters and what helps us refine our thinking. A simple set of questions can help distinguish between what is useless and what is worthy of incorporating into our mental models.

Our portals to information include mainstream media, individuals, feeds, news aggregators, and social media algorithms. We need to manage these as a portfolio, maximizing the diversity and balance that will support our purpose. Digital, print, audio, and video formats each have their own strengths for sense-making, but the right balance depends largely on personal preferences.

Curating information not just for ourselves, but also for others, provides a powerful guide for our filtering and sense-making. Filtering is not just about seeking information; setting guidelines to assess—or even preempt—inbound flows is a vital part of keeping us sane.

I n the late 1940s Claude Shannon lived in a small apartment in Greenwich Village a short walk from his Bell Labs office, frequented jazz clubs, and stayed out late. After he took an axe to his piano to stoke his fire one cold winter, his most cherished remaining possessions were his record player and his clarinet. His loud music annoyed his fellow tenants but led to a passionate romance when his intelligent and vivacious downstairs neighbor knocked on his door to ask him to turn it down. In between his worldly diversions, in Shannon's intense hours working in his office and scribbling ideas on napkins, he created a new field of science, information theory.[2]

Bell System was then the monopoly provider of telephone and telegraph service across the United States. At the time, the quality of phone conversations was highly variable, with background noise sometimes making it hard to hear what people were saying. Shannon's theory was centered on maximizing the signal-to-noise ratio, the proportion of useful information to meaningless noise transmitted over a channel. His broader thesis transformed how we think about information, for the first time positing it as something measurable, and in the process inventing the concept of the "bit" as the elemental unit of information, a concept that underlies the entire digital age.

We now all intuitively understand the personal relevance of a signal-to-noise ratio. In the internet and social media age the amount of "noise," which essentially means information with zero value, has soared exponentially, far beyond the amount of "signal," referring to information of value. It is becoming harder to identify what matters to us amid the unlimited effluvia of today's web.

Simply taking in more information will not yield more signal. "The more data you get, the less you know what's going on," observes author and philosopher Nassim Nicholas Taleb.[3]

We urgently need to refine our ability to filter information, which is as much about effortlessly ignoring what is not relevant to us as it is about picking out the pearls from the dross. Venture capital doyen Brad Feld notes that, "I can't consume signal 100 percent of the time (or my head would explode), so I let plenty of noise creep in, but I've got very effectively tunable noise filters. Anyone involved in the entrepreneurial ecosystem should ponder this—I encourage you to focus on amplifying signal, not noise."[4]

Beyond Overwhelm

Our senses send around 11 million bits of information per second to our brain, yet our conscious minds can only process what has been variously estimated at 40 to 200 bits per second.[5] We could not function without our brain's highly refined ability to filter only the most relevant signals from a universe of sensory input.

The result of "the reducing valve of the brain and nervous system" is "a measly trickle of the kind of consciousness which will help us to stay alive," observes the great writer Aldous Huxley.[6] Our brain's filtering mechanisms are designed to protect us. Conditions such as ADHD, schizophrenia, and autism are often associated with atypical filtering that can result in painful sensory overwhelm.

Yet attenuated sensory filtering has also been linked to creativity and the ability to experience at times intense perceptions of beauty. We need to limit the onslaught on our senses, yet there is deep danger from over filtering. Today many people seem to notice little around them, living lives of deep routine, immured from the world save for what comes to them through their digital devices. Their constrained perception restricts not just what they see, but every aspect of their thinking, experience, and lives.

Effectively filtering out the irrelevant while noticing what matters is a skill fundamental to survival and success. While our individual neurophysiology can help or hinder this, we can tap our brains' neuroplasticity to improve our sensory-filtering capabilities.[7] We do not need to accept how our inbuilt filtering mechanisms work by default. "The art of seeing has to be learned," novelist Marguerite Duras reminds us.[8]

What Information Serves You?

Immersed in information, we need to judiciously apply both technological and cognitive filters. To do that we require criteria for assessing what should pass through our filters and what should be ignored. In Chapter 1 you considered your purposes for engaging with information. Knowing these provides valuable guidance, yet by themselves they may not yield clarity on what specifically merits your precious attention.

My old friend Karl-Erik Sveiby incisively observed over 20 years ago that while some information has value, a great deal of information in fact has negative value, when the cost of the time and effort of consuming a piece of information is greater than what it brings you.[9] Even more so if it is misleading, inaccurate, or outright false, as is now depressingly common. We need to be able to assess whether any given information has positive or negative value for us, based on our unique circumstances and intentions.

The ability to discern the information that best serves you shapes the quality of your life.

Information serves us if it helps us to understand the world better, make better decisions, and live more fulfilled lives, even in the smallest way. Information does not serve us well if it misleads us, reinforces our biases, makes us unhappy, or simply wastes our time and attention by being irrelevant to our intentions.

Your knowledge frameworks are the foundation of your mental models, thinking, and decisions. As you saw in Chapter 2, any new information should be assessed relative to your frameworks, in whether they fit well, refine your thinking, or provide new evidence to consider.

We also need to heed the impact of information on our mood and emotions. Many studies have demonstrated a correlation between depression and overuse of social media.[10] The word "doomscrolling," describing compulsively following upsetting news, was first used in 2018. Two years later the rise of Covid-19 made it an accurate description of how we all behaved, earning it an accolade of "word of the year."[11]

The reality is almost all reported news is negative, and most "good news" initiatives have failed abysmally. Yet we can tend to avoid what distresses us and turn to what we find encouraging or inspiring. Make a point of noticing the influence on your mood as you consume different kinds of news. As you can, tend toward what uplifts you and away from what adversely impacts you. Simple behavior changes can make a big difference.

When you seek to identify whether information serves you well, the most important consideration is if it enhances your mental models. You must be highly aware of whether information fits with your current thinking. Identifying data that supports your thinking is natural and can be useful. However, you also need to seek the most interesting evidence that could show that what you believe might, in fact, not be precisely true. We need to overcome our inbuilt inclination to seek validation.

Transcending Bias

In the late 1960s the gifted and ebullient Amos Tversky gave a presentation at the Hebrew University of Jerusalem where he taught on how people take in new information, proposing they were usually rational. In the audience was the self-professed pessimist Daniel Kahneman, who told Tversky, "Brilliant talk, but I don't believe a word of it," submitting that our judgments are likely as prone to error as our highly fallible senses.[12]

This sparked one of the seminal scientific collaborations of the last century, with the pair introducing the concept of "cognitive bias" to the world, cataloguing in detail the manifold failings of our minds to accurately perceive the world around us. After Tversky's death, Kahneman received the Nobel Prize for the groundbreaking advances the duo had made in uncovering the nature of our brains.

In short, they brought to light that humans do not see the world as it is, with many inbuilt biases leading us to an incorrect understanding of what is around us. Some biases are quite simple, such as primacy and recency bias, which result in us being more likely to remember the first and last things that we see or hear in a sequence. More central to the distortions in which we process information are those that support our preconceptions.

Likely the most fundamental and most insidious bias is confirmation bias, which leads us to perceive and give importance to information that supports our prior views, and to ignore, downplay, or simply not see evidence that contradicts our opinions. Dozens of studies have verified the phenomenon, but you don't need to read them; I'm sure you see this phenomenon amply demonstrated by those around you. Yet it is one thing to notice it in others, another to see it in yourself. At the center of Kahneman's work is the observation, "it is easier to recognize other people's mistakes than our own."[13]

In the parlance of cognitive psychology shared in Kahneman's *Thinking, Fast and Slow*, we need System 2—our deliberative mind—to regularly override System 1—our responsive mind. This cannot and does not need to be through every moment of the day. The reality is that much of our cognition and behavior is driven by habit and intuition. Yet when actively filtering information, we should strive to be conscious, aware we inevitably have cognitive biases that constrain our ability to integrate pertinent information. We need to deliberately seek out evidence that will improve our mental models and decisions.

Probabilistic Thinking

Thomas Bayes spent his working life as a church minister in eighteenth-century southern England. During his life he also managed to write two papers, one on theology and the other on mathematics. It was only after his death that his unpublished work on probability was passed on to a friend, who marshaled it through the process of presenting it to the Royal Society. Two hundred and fifty years later Bayes's work is considered more relevant than ever and has become deeply embedded in Silicon Valley culture.[14]

Bayes's theorem describes the probability that a given event will occur. The heart of the approach is to start with an estimated probability, using whatever means available, and then updating the probability based on all new information. The model has extensive applications beyond statistical analysis, notably in finance, medicine, and genetics, and is now used extensively in building machine learning models, which are designed to keep improving based on additional information.

The impact of Bayes's work goes far beyond the mathematicians that apply it. It represents a frame of mind of actively seeking new information. It is founded on the assumption that current thinking can be improved. In the book *Superforecasting*, which studies the small minority who excel at forecasting complex events, the authors note that "what matters far more to the super-forecasters than Bayes' theorem is Bayes' core insight of gradually getting closer to the truth by constantly updating in proportion to the weight of the evidence."[15]

One of the most powerful shifts you can make is from convictions to probabilistic thinking.

Bayesian thinking is in essence continuously seeking new information so you can enhance your assessment of a situation. This is called a "Bayesian update," or more bluntly for humans, a "belief revision." As you saw in Chapter 2, a prediction or attribution of a probability provides a valuable filter for any new information, highlighting what is pertinent and allowing refinement of the underlying thinking. Thinking in terms of likelihoods means that when you encounter new information, you can move beyond considering whether it supports or contradicts your views, to assessing its impact on the probabilities you attribute to your theses.

Look for Surprises

In a similar way to predictive text on your smartphone, your brain is continually building expectations for what comes next. If what happens is close enough to what it anticipates, its response is minimal. If, however, a word, sound, image, or idea is unexpected, the brain generates an N400 electrical pulse, so called because it has a negative potential and peaks 400 milliseconds after the event.

N400 is essentially a signal of surprise. Neuroscientists John Kounios and Mark Beeman, whom you will meet again later in this book, explain that "we continuously build mental models of the world around us—our boxes—to help predict what will happen next. Any deviation from these expectations causes a group of neurons to shout in synchrony to signal that something is different, unexpected, or just wrong. And those brainwaves aren't pointless alarms. They are critical to the brain's efforts to keep itself current and accurate."[16]

While we are afflicted with cognitive biases, our brain also tries to alert us when our mental models may be wrong. We must pay attention. "A capacity for surprise is an essential aspect of our mental life, and surprise itself is the most sensitive indication of how we understand our world and what we expect from it," says Kahneman.

> *Surprises are immensely more valuable*
> *than finding what you expect.*

As we scan our information sources, we need to be most keenly attuned to what does *not* fit with our frameworks and mental models. In Chapter 2 you learned how to use your frameworks to identify signals of what does and doesn't fit with your models. As you daily soak in information, your first priority is finding what is both surprising and credible.

The Time Value of Information

It seems the vast majority of people spend their days checking the latest news. However, one useful rule of thumb to assess the potential value of information is its age. Most of the news that comes out today will have almost zero value or importance past tomorrow. Nassim Nicholas Taleb says "to be completely cured of newspapers, spend a year reading the previous week's newspapers."[17] Doing this highlights the unimportance and transience of the vast majority of the news.

In contrast, articles, books, or other content that still receives attention weeks, months, or years later is far more likely to offer lasting value. If you are seeking to improve your thinking, prioritize content that has withstood the test of time over continuously scanning for the latest updates. Books and other deeply thoughtful content are still the best source of expert, insightful thinking to learn or enhance your mental models.

Spend more time with content of proven value than you do with today's ephemera.

If the bulk of your information activities are in scanning (and rescanning) the latest news, you will only be skimming the surface. Certainly, to keep abreast of change you need to scour for relevant updates as well as indulge in deeper dives into rich troves. Yet more than ever that is an activity fraught with danger, as misinformation, disinformation, and just straight-out bullshit fills our information sources.

Finding Gems Amid Bullshit

When University of Washington launched its Calling Bullshit in the Age of Big Data course in 2017, its 160-student capacity was booked out in one minute flat.[18] The first course objective is to "remain vigilant for bullshit contaminating your information diet," something we all need to be highly conscious of given its lavish presence in what we consume. Massive interest in the program has led to online courses for high school children and educators and an excellent book by the course instructors, Carl Bergstrom and Jevin West.[19]

Not just spotting bullshit, but also positively identifying high-value information, must be core capabilities for everyone today. Since filtering has become so much harder, we need to apply our critical faculties using a content-filtering framework, as shown in Figure 3.1. There are three domains on which we need to focus: you, the source, and the content itself.

- Is this relevant and important to you?
- Do you have any preconceptions on this topic?
- Do you want it to be true (or false)?

YOU

- How reputable is the publication?
- How credible is the author?
- Might they have any bias you should take into account?

SOURCE

- Is the detailed rationale reasonable?
- Are quoted sources reputable and accurately represented?
- Do other authoritative sources corroborate?

CONTENT

FIGURE 3.1 A Content Filtering Framework

Only you can assess the potential value of any given piece of content. The essential first question is whether it is sufficiently relevant to you to pay attention at all. We should appraise any information before making it part of our mental models, but we can only spend that time on what is important.

As we grow to understand cognitive bias, we need to be highly attentive to whether we *want* new information to be true. It is safe to assume you have political opinions. If you are like the vast majority of people, you gravitate more to articles that point to the deficiencies of politicians you don't like than those you support. I'm certainly not immune. Being aware of our preconceptions allows us to be more critical in assessing content, whether it supports our views or conflicts with them.

A ready heuristic for the quality of content is the source, but we should also understand this is not an unfailing measure. The most credible newspapers in the world make mistakes, despite sometimes rigorous fact-checking standards, and editors are humans not immune to championing their beliefs. Even publication in a reputable scientific journal, which entails a thorough peer review, does not mean findings are correct. To take just *Nature*, by some measures the world's most reputable journal, there were 49 retractions of published articles in the decade to 2021, and that doesn't mean that every other article was completely correct.[20]

It makes sense to filter for credibility at least as much by individual author as by publication. Many media outlets aggregate a broad range of content, sometimes to spark debate rather than as an endorsement. Develop opinions on who you consider reliable or untrustworthy.

On the other hand, you should treat with caution ideas from an unknown publication or author, and indeed verify that they are the source they profess. For years one of the major sources of shared misinformation was a website mimicking the URL and appearance of ABC News. Yet great ideas can come from outside the mainstream, so being unknown is not disqualifying.

Finally, you need to assess the content itself, going beyond the headline to the content, which is sometimes clearly satire or with deeply flawed logic. Most important of all, you need wherever possible to reference the original sources, or cross-check with other authorities.

Go to the Ultimate Source

Once, while searching for some data, I found an infographic containing a startling statistic. I was intrigued about the data point and where it came from, so scoured through the long list of references at the bottom of the chart, finding another infographic with the statistic, then in turn another. Following the thread eventually led me back to the original source. I had apparently stumbled upon an infernal loop of references to what appeared to be an invented data point with no credible provenance.

The most powerful single behavior to ensure you get quality information is developing the habit of always going to the source. You can be confident that most of what you find on the web has not been traced to the source by those sharing it. When cheap and quick content creation is the name of the game, no one bothers to check whether something they have seen is actually correct, creating an amplification loop in which any distortion—or sometimes invention—begins to be taken as gospel.

For anything important, always try to track back to the original information source.

I can't tell you how many times in the course of researching this book I found a quote, anecdote, or statistic that was intriguing, which upon investigation either had been massively distorted or simply did not have an identifiable source. If you truly want to be well informed, any time you see something that interests or surprises you, endeavor to find the original source of the information and decide whether you trust where it came from. This is one of the most valuable information habits you can develop.

Of course, before we assess information, we need to choose the founts from which we drink. The ongoing fragmentation of information markets has afforded us a variety of portals to access our mental sustenance.

Selecting Your Portals

The visionary Marshall McLuhan decades ago insightfully described the media as an extension of our senses. You used to be only able to see and hear what was immediately around you. With hordes of professional journalists now complemented by billions of people brandishing powerful digital devices, every camera and microphone in the world extends your senses to whatever those armies experience and share.

We can now access much of the entire universe of information available, if we choose to bypass the now archaic filters imposed by mainstream media. The challenge is that this unleashes a tsunami of noise that inevitably drowns out the signals that matter to us.

It is not just information that has proliferated, but also the ways we can access it. We now have a wealth of options to learn what is happening. Rather than sources, we should think about "portals," the doorways through which we discover information, each with distinctive characteristics in how they filter and aggregate inputs. Our five primary portals to information are shown in Figure 3.2.

As the diagram illustrates, you can sometimes directly experience what is new. However, it is a very big world and you cannot be everywhere, so you will uncover much of what is new through media or the direct reporting of individuals. Media and individuals (if we can even distinguish between them these days) are our sources. In our increasingly disintegrated media landscape, we don't necessarily go directly to these sources. In many cases we discover what is interesting to us through aggregators or feeds.

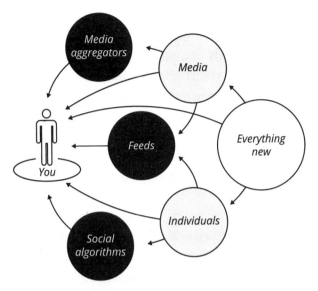

FIGURE 3.2 Your Portals to Information

There is a critical distinction between feeds where we select the inputs and those that are shaped by algorithms. As we will see, sometimes those algorithms can be very useful, but in other cases they dramatically distort what we see and thus how we perceive the world. In the diagram, feeds can bring together both media sources and individuals. Media aggregators and social media are both based on algorithms, so it is important to understand how these algorithms select what they present to you and the implications for their role in your media diet.

Let us examine each of the portals through which you can access your information diet and how best to use them. First, we need to consider how to build a portfolio of information portals and sources that will best support your objectives.

Diverse Information Portfolios

Modern portfolio theory lies at the center of contemporary investment management. Originally proposed in 1952 by Harry Markowitz, who won a Nobel Prize for his insight, it remains in the core curriculum of every finance course. In essence it proves that if your portfolio is diversified, containing a range of investments that are not highly correlated in their performance, you will achieve a better overall return for the risk you take. Markowitz had mathematically verified the age-old adage "don't put all your eggs in one basket."

This principle also applies to other domains, including the information sources we use. In particular, there is a deep risk to our mental models in drawing on a narrow set of sources, especially those that are overly aligned in their political, social, or epistemic outlooks. There is more than one way to look at anything. We should adopt as a core precept the adage of influential social scientist Gregory Bateson: "Knowledge comes from but a single perspective; wisdom comes from multiple perspectives."[21]

This might be most obviously the case in politics, where anything can be viewed through the diverse lenses of partisan beliefs. If all your input comes from sources with aligned political stances, it is almost impossible to form opinions that reflect your unique views and identity.

Less obviously, science also requires multiple frames. Some domains of science are essentially settled and agreed upon. As we push back the boundaries of our scientific knowledge, and sometimes come back to question what is already seen as established, brisk—or sometimes acrimonious—debates between thinkers are an integral part of advancing our collective understanding.

People who follow only a handful of prominent techno-optimists might believe that technology will inevitably cure the ills of society. Perhaps describing a greater proportion of the population, people who are continuously exposed to dire news about social and environmental issues may not ever see that there are potential solutions to the pressing problems of today.

The single most important factor in selecting your information sources is diversity.

The challenge and opportunity are to include highly varied sources in our regular information diet. In 2015 I started compiling a list of leading female futurists across all continents. The intent was to provide a resource for myself and others to identify incisive viewpoints beyond the usual suspects.[22] You can find or compile for yourself similar lists of individuals or media outlets that offer thinking outside the mainstream. Where possible, include the most thoughtful sources that are likely to challenge your outlook.

Media

An increasing proportion of people never turn to a specific news site or broadcast program to find out what's going on in the world. They find relevant news through social media, news aggregators, or their friends sharing links with them. Academics describe the phenomenon of not actively seeking news as the News Finds Me (NFM) perception.[23] While it can be used as a pejorative term, some of the most insightful and informed people I know essentially let information find them. "My approach is that things come by, and if they keep coming by, they're probably important," says Tim O'Reilly.[24]

Those who were reading news-on-paper when they came of age are more likely to continue to go directly to a media brand they know and trust, whether they access it through the web, paper, television, or radio. Members of younger generations often only access media sources indirectly, through social media or aggregators.[25] If done thoughtfully that can provide an excellent range of relevant updates, but for many there is a place for accessing selected media directly.

Delegating Your Filtering

Do you want to read the same thing as many billionaires? Bill Gates, Warren Buffett, and many of their peers consistently read the *Wall Street Journal*, the *New York Times*, and the *Economist*.

They are delegating part of their information filtering, selection, and prioritization to the editors of those august publications. They absolutely use other media and sources, but as a starting point they believe those publications will provide solid coverage of the news that matters as well as useful context to those stories.

The promise of almost every mainstream news publication or program has been that it tells you what you need to know. By consuming it you are trusting the decisions of those editors on what news to include and how it is framed. Pre-internet that meant using a news source was in fact choosing who selected the news for you. Now that we have a plethora of news providers, the primary reason to go directly to the front page of a publication is either that you find value in its editorial choices or you trust the way it covers those stories.

The value can also be in understanding how that publication's audience sees the world. Investor Josh Wolfe says his wife makes fun of him for reading *USA Today* in addition to all the "serious" newspapers. He responds, "Well, I need to read *USA Today* because I need to know whatever X million Americans are waking up in Marriotts and being influenced by."[26] I have never owned a television, but when I have time free in a hotel room, I may turn to news channels that I wouldn't normally see to discover what millions are watching.

Your selection of consistent news sources inevitably shapes you and how you see the world. You need to be conscious in those choices, and open to changing them if your priorities shift or the sources don't fulfil their promised value to you.

Individuals

The rapid rise of the newsletter service Substack, which hit over 1 million paying subscribers in late 2021, points to a structural shift in how people filter information: they increasingly prefer to go to individuals rather than media institutions. The first wave of individual media came from blogging, online video, content-driven social networks, and podcasting. Now that a sufficient audience is proving happy to support creators directly, the media landscape is fragmenting even more.

This is an opportunity to be more granular in our sources by selecting people we trust. We can also simply choose to follow only individuals within larger media organizations by using feeds and filters. However, primarily going to individuals rather than media sources offers a heightened danger of being exposed only to those who think like you. Make sure to include the most thoughtful people with whom you disagree.

Investing in Your Personal Information Networks

My last corporate role before leaving to launch my own ventures was as global director of capital markets at Thomson Financial, which later merged with Reuters to form Thomson Reuters. My team provided real-time reporting and analysis on the global primary debt markets. Market participants were the source of essentially all our information. They shared it with us because of our relationships of trust. We engaged daily in barter of updates on what was happening behind the scenes in the markets, and more importantly, shared context and diverse perspectives on the transactions.

For many jobs "know-who" is as or more important than "know-how." If you know who to ask, you don't need the knowledge yourself. It is not just a question of knowing who to ask; it requires a relationship that results in people taking the time and effort to help you. Networks of knowledge are also networks of trust and reciprocity.

Top-ranked analyst and author R "Ray" Wang delves deep into technology trends and their implications. For that he relies on his personal networks. "The bigger your network, the more likely you can find someone within that network or at least a couple of degrees of separation," he says. If there is a topic he wants to dive into, he reaches out to whoever in his network is most likely to give him the insights he needs.

Wang says the reason they accept his request for a meeting is to "pay it forward" within extended groups in which value is freely exchanged. "In case you have a question, or you want to know something, or whether it's a job hunt, or whether it's a tip, or whether something's coming your way, there's enough self-interest for you to want to be part of one of those groups," he says.[27]

This is described as "diffuse reciprocity," in which you engage in mutual value exchange, not with individuals, but with members of a broader community. You might help someone who will help someone else who will help you. If you want to be able to tap the insights of the world's top experts in a particular field, you should start by helping people like them where you can. If you assist others in their pursuit of insight, this will flow back to you. And of course, wherever possible, if you have a conversation, you want everyone involved to get at least as much value from it as you.

> *People can be your greatest source of insight, but for that, you need to invest in your personal information networks.*

Leading venture capitalist Fred Wilson's personal network is central to how he uncovers useful information. "I have several dozen friends who are always sending me things to read or watch or listen to," he writes. "Many/most of these people do not work in tech but are hyper-curious and have great breadth of interest. They are my most valuable source of content and inspiration and I have cultivated these relationships over my entire adult life. This was not calculated or planned. It just happened." His view is that "technology shows me things I already know about. Humans show me things I don't know about."[28]

Sometimes we might call or message the right person directly, but today much of the insight being shared is within closed groups on platforms such as WhatsApp, WeChat, Telegram, and Signal. Insightful viewpoints on the topics of the moment can be found in voice conversations on Discord or Clubhouse, where Silicon Valley elite led the way for a diverse range of interesting thinkers to share their perspectives, often for anyone who cares to tune in.

Feeds

Dave Winer prefers the description "media hacker" to software developer, though software is his medium for impact. In 1994, soon after the World Wide Web was created, Winer helped San Francisco newspaper strikers automate their landmark online news site *San Francisco Free Press*.[29] His company UserLand Software followed up by launching the first user-friendly platform for blogging in 1997. Winer began developing a content-sharing protocol he called "Really Simple Syndication," or RSS.

In 2000 Adam Curry, who had been a prominent VJ on MTV, flew into New York and invited Dave Winer to meet him in his room in what Winer describes as a "fancy rock star type hotel." Curry passionately described his vision for a world in which not just blogs but also radio, music, other audio, or video could be distributed to the world. Winer was intrigued and adapted RSS to include an enclosure for audio. On January 20, 2001, the inauguration day of George W. Bush, Winer launched a feed containing *U.S. Blues*, Grateful Dead's biting song on the state of America, to create the first audio RSS feed.[30] Two decades later, people listen to over 15 billion hours of podcasts every year, largely subscribed to through RSS feeds.

Syndication is a foundational element of the digital economy, enabling us to subscribe to receive updates whenever our favorite news sites, bloggers, podcasters, or video producers share new content. Services such as Twitter, Instagram, and their ilk at their core are feeds to follow the updates of people who interest you.

Finding 20 Good People

Technology evangelist and author Robert Scoble's primary interface to information is Twitter interface Tweetdeck. Nestled among the seemingly boundless inanity on Twitter, many of the world's leaders in their fields, in technology, media, science, and of course politics, share their insights, work, perspectives, and the most interesting content they encounter. To help us find the treasures amid the drivel, the list function of Twitter lets us define topics within which we only see the tweets of those we respect.

The issue is selecting who you follow. "You have to get to know the people you're listening to. And that takes time," says Scoble. "Make a list of 20 people that are really baller in this industry or the topic. If you're trying to learn how to do pottery, you'd better know who Lynda Weinman is, she should be one of the 20 people on your list. And if she's not, she will be pretty quick once you start building a list like this, because you'll find the other 19 and then they'll start saying, 'hey, look at Lynda's stuff.' The world starts pointing you at these people, and that gets you up to date."[31]

Many of the information masters I interviewed for this book mentioned numbers around 20 as a guideline scope for their tightly curated lists. "It's a little bit of a shotgun approach to start with," says "personal knowledge mastery" instructor Harold Jarche. "Start paying attention to what they're doing. You can tune those signals; you can amplify the ones that are giving you good information, and you can decrease the noisy ones."

Early in the Covid-19 pandemic Jarche created a Twitter list with just a dozen highly diverse sources he trusts who have all "gone a little bit against the mainstream." He has added and taken away from this list but kept it contained. "Finding your limits becomes important as well. If you're spending all your time seeking and reading, and not doing anything about it, that's not very helpful."[32]

Setting Up Feeds

To bring together your selected sources you can draw on a wide range of RSS readers—for example, Feedly, Inoreader, or Newsblur.

Some readers have useful features beyond simple aggregation, such as AI content selection, integration with note-taking apps, or filtering content by author or category.

You can also use platforms such as Google News to set up alert feeds for specific terms appearing in the news—for example, topics relating to your field of expertise. These surface all news items that include your terms. The risk is that these often provide too many results from sources of highly varied quality.

Social data innovator Marshall Kirkpatrick has set up (and shares on the web) Google custom search engines that each return results only from a curated set of sources. Rather than go to the entire web he can search within the sites he trusts. To ensure he draws on diverse sources he searches within Twitter lists he has created of underrepresented groups, such as Indigenous leaders and women in tech.[33]

Newsletter subscriptions are effectively feeds into your email inbox, though you can use software tools to direct all your newsletters to a separate reader. Leslie Shannon, who works for Nokia scouting for relevant technology trends, uses newsletters extensively. "I'm paying somebody else to do the scanning for me . . . except the newsletters are free," she says. The issue is in discovering and selecting which ones to read. "I will look at everything once," she reports, but only to assess them. "I'm an unsubscribe monster . . . ruthless so that the things that come into my inbox, I know are things that I want to pay attention to."[34]

Algorithmic Input

Rampant technology has largely created the alarming surfeit of information we experience. But could the solution be in the problem? Can technology not also guide us to the information that is the most relevant to us? If the extraordinary capabilities of AI can be applied to learning our interests, it should be able to direct us to the information that will best serve us. The problem? Most algorithms are developed and applied, not to serve us, but to exploit us.

Algorithms can be immensely valuable in helping us identify the information we need. But we need to be very careful how we use algorithmic information discovery in recognizing the design intention of the algorithms as well as their quality. Algorithms shape what you see in your social media newsfeeds and on media aggregators, but the way they work in each channel is very different.

Social Algorithms

Yuval Noah Harari, author of bestselling books including *Sapiens*, does not mince words in describing the impact of social media algorithms. "Once you have an external outlier that understands you better than you understand yourself, liberal democracy as we have known it for the last century or so is doomed," he says.[35]

In November 2020, 48 percent of Americans aged 18–29 and 40 percent of 30–49-year-olds reported that social media was the most common way they accessed election news. Not surprisingly, these respondents proved to be less knowledgeable than others about current events and politics.[36]

Most social media sites are based around their newsfeed, where their constantly refined algorithmic selections of content are crafted to make you spend more time on the site, engage with posts, come back frequently, and click on paid advertisements.

The realization that Facebook was exploiting negative emotions such as anger and envy to increase engagement is one of the factors prompting many millions to leave the site over the past years.[37] Yet many still find social media sites useful for a range of reasons, including keeping in touch with old friends.

For those who still find value on social media platforms, there are a few things you can do to give yourself a modicum of control. One way is to block the newsfeed entirely. Over 200,000 people have downloaded News Feed Eradicator, a browser extension that replaces the newsfeed of multiple major social networks with inspiring quotes, leaving all other functionality intact. There are, unfortunately, very limited options to edit the newsfeed on most social media services, save for Twitter where you can choose to see the most recent posts from those you follow rather than those selected by the platform.

Where you still have a degree of control is simply in only engaging with people or posts that you want to see more of in your stream. You can make people you follow more or less likely to appear through blocking or temporarily snoozing them. Never engage with content that gives you negative emotions such as outrage. If you do, you are falling into their trap and will see more things that enrage you. That is not a useful state of mind. If people share clickbait content, take them out of your stream; they are taking precious attention from you. More generally, it is safe to recommend that you minimize your engagement on social media.

Media Aggregators
What do Meta CEO Mark Zuckerberg and Google CEO Sundar Pichai have in common? One thing is that they both rely on technology news site Techmeme to keep on top of the latest news in the industry, along with many of the top tech leaders and venture capitalists in Silicon Valley and beyond.[38] The Techmeme page displays a constantly updated list of the most important news in the sector, based on the extent of discussion by those most influential in the community. If you are in tech, a visit to the site efficiently updates you on the latest news and offers reassurance that you're not missing anything important.

The advent of Google News and more recently Apple News offers easy access to a compilation of news from a wide variety of publications that is sufficient for many people to feel they know what they need. Those who wish can dive into specific categories such as national politics, local news, science, sports, or even more precise tranches. These kinds of aggregators are primarily useful for anyone who just wants to be broadly aware of what's happening in the world. One advantage is that the primary stream shows news across all categories, not just the ones you tend to follow, exposing you to a quick but broad view of what's going on. However, they should not be considered sufficient for those wanting to go beyond the superficial.

User-driven aggregators such as Reddit's subreddit groups and Hacker News for the startup community, which use algorithms based on member votes, can provide a useful view of what's new and interesting on those topics. The comments sections, which also apply user voting to highlight the best and bury the worst, can at times provide thought-provoking perspectives.

Despite literally hundreds of attempts at creating personalized news aggregators in the hope of attracting legions of readers seeking a distillation of the news, most have hit the dust, many of them deservedly. I have long been disappointed in the personalization quality of the available news aggregators, though I hold hopes for the new emerging generation of tools.

Building Your Information Portfolio

Popular internet culture columnist Taylor Lorenz, writing for the *New York Times* and then the *Washington Post*, has a media diet that matches her distinctive job. "I'm basically consuming information all day on whatever app I'm using," she reports. "I follow lots of Instagram accounts, check out the Explore page, spend about an hour or two per day on TikTok or watching YouTube."

She looks to her community for content recommendations. "I have a Twitter list of people I follow and just read whatever links they tweet out that seem interesting. I also read links dropped in a variety of group chats and Slack groups." Other than selected news recap podcasts, she goes consistently to only one publication, reading the *Daily Mail* homepage "top to bottom several times per day."[39]

Your information portfolio will likely be markedly different from Lorenz's. Yet, as she has, you need to establish a consistent set of portals and habits that support your objectives. These will include daily routines as well as some sources accessed less regularly.

Consider a long-term cryptocurrency investor. To meet her information needs, she will likely set up feeds from the major specialist crypto news services or potentially consistently visit a few of the sites directly, complementing this with subscriptions to a handful of the most insightful sector newsletters. Since many crypto pundits and experts are on Twitter, she will keep an eye on a list compiled by someone she respects or set up her own list of those she finds most intriguing.

If she is concerned about the outlook for cryptocurrency regulation, she will set up a web-wide alert for specific search terms, or a narrower filter drawing only relevant news from a set of credible mainstream publications. She may regularly visit one of the online communities where the core crypto developers hang out to keep abreast of progress on the crypto platform road maps.

A sophisticated supply chain executive will have a very different portfolio, including a dashboard of internal information on the state of the company's logistics, headlines from major news outlets across different regions of the world, industry-specific sections of media aggregators, and perhaps major weather alerts. He will also have a feed or selected set of sources to keep informed on the latest developments in transport, warehousing, sensor technology, 3D printing, and other advances that may impact his operations; however, he will most likely check this less frequently.

Review your information purposes and start with a blank slate. If you were setting up your information portfolio from scratch, what portals would be most important? Which outlets, if any, are worth going to directly? Can any media aggregators be useful, perhaps with some setup? If you choose to build feeds of media or individuals, how will you select the sources? Should social media play a role other than for your socializing?

As for financial portfolios, you should regularly rebalance depending on the demands of your role and continual reassessment of the quality and value of the information you are getting. Beyond the portals and sources you choose, you also need to intelligently select the media formats that suit you.

Your Mix of Media Formats

The rise of digital communication has yielded a cornucopia of ways to consume information, education, and entertainment. None of these options replaces old favorites such as print, television, and radio, but add to them to offer us myriad choices.

In the same way that we need to be conscious in filtering, we should make deliberate choices on the media formats we use, rather than rely on the default of what is easy or habitual. There is no optimal prescription for the balance of formats because it is a deeply personal choice. It depends not only on your cognitive style and preferences, but also on your daily routine, the devices you use, and when you choose to engage with information.

Don't assume that what you're doing now is the best way. Try different approaches and see if you can find better alternatives. Let's consider the factors that drive your selection of media formats across the major alternatives of print, audio, video, and a proliferating assortment of digital screens.

Choosing Your Media

There are in essence two types of media: those that let us choose our pace and those that lock our attention to the flow. Part of the magic of the written word is that you can vary your reading pace from very fast to very slow, depending on how deeply you wish to engage with the text. Books, newspapers, newsletters, and articles can be absorbed in precisely the way that suits you.

With audio or video, you are locked to the pace it unfolds. Many people speed up audio, using exercise or commuting time to listen to podcasts or articles. Untrained people are rarely comfortable beyond one and a half times normal speed, though vision-impaired people and some who have undertaken specific training can listen with good comprehension to audio at triple or more normal speed.[40] Listening faster is not necessarily better, since it consumes more attention (which is fine for the gym but not highly compatible with some other tasks such as driving) and can induce stress. The point is to thrive, not to make your information intake unpleasant.

Audio is certainly a viable substitute to text; however, often the real value of audio and video are in their greater emotional engagement and thus ability to integrate into your thinking. Compare the impact of watching or listening to Martin Luther King Jr.'s "I Have a Dream" speech to that of reading it. I find I register insights when listening to podcasts that I miss when reading the transcripts.

Print Versus Screen

Print on paper boasts a plethora of advantages, including zero boot time, high legibility in varied lighting, pleasing aesthetics, no need to recharge, tolerance to beach and bath conditions, and not disrupting airplane navigation systems. Indeed, our lasting love for print books suggests they will be with us for decades to come. In 2021 over 825 million print books were sold in the United States, the most since the rise of e-books, and more than four times digital format sales.[41] For a little while yet we can also opt to read major newspapers on paper, and we can print out digital content if we choose.

Indeed, while the many studies comparing comprehension from reading print and digital formats yield varied results, they tend to come down on the side of print, largely due to superior visual ergonomics.[42] In addition, reading print is inherently a more focused format than on digital devices, which all too readily allow our attention to stray.

On the other hand, digital texts offer myriad advantages, not least in being able to search through all the notes, articles, and books you have read, copy phrases into other documents, and of particular delight to frequent travelers, carry an unlimited number of books on expeditions.

Since note-taking is vital to comprehension and assimilation, a key factor in selecting reading format is how well it suits your approach to note-taking. Blogger and curator Maria Popova recently renamed her website The Marginalian, referring to taking notes in the margins of books. Yet she reads in digital formats, exporting her notes to Evernote for sense-making and searching.[43]

Venture capitalist Marc Andreessen reads print extensively, shaping how he highlights the text. "When there's something interesting in the book I underline it," he says. "And then if it's really interesting, I dog-ear the page that it's on. And then there's a few books that I've read where it's like, they destabilize the piles of books because I've dog-eared every single page and now the book is crooked. And the books on top of it will, like, tip over at some point."[44]

Many people find that they can more easily reference and recall notes in print books, since our cognition often uses spatial references. Investment strategist Michael Mauboussin reports that "my own mental recall tends to do much better with physical assets than it does with electronic. Even though I know I could search for it electronically, I feel more comfortable with it in the physical form."[45]

Information Is More than Content

You may have heard the oft-quoted phrase that "a weekday edition of the *New York Times* contains more information than the average person was likely to come across in a lifetime in 17th century England."[46] A startling statement, and utter rubbish. In fact, the average Englishman of a few hundred years ago may have soaked in more information about his environment each day than most Americans of the early twenty-first century, by actually perceiving what was around him rather than filtering out everything but the mobile phone screen in front of him. It's just that the information he came across wasn't necessarily contained in words or videos.

If you limit your understanding of the world to what you can read or watch on a screen, you will have no true knowledge. Certainly, we need to draw on the information and insights from the oceans of media that we can access. But the most insightful people actively look around them every day for the signals that help them make sense of the world.

Landing in Bangkok on his travels as a marketer for a tooth-paste brand, Dietrich Mateschitz hopped on a tuk-tuk motorcycle rickshaw to get through the traffic-bound city. He noticed that all the drivers were drinking the same beverage to keep awake through their long days. He reached out to the owner of the company, negotiated worldwide rights, and launched Red Bull, which now sells almost 8 billion cans a year, more than one for every person on the planet.[47]

The Power of Curation

In medieval England a curate was responsible for the care of the souls of those in his parish, guiding them to the messages that would lead to their salvation. In following centuries, "curator" began to be used to describe those selecting the most worthy art to appear on the walls of museums.

It was only in the 1990s that cultural aspirants appropriated the word to describe the selection of DJs at a nightclub, sneakers in a shoe store, books of the month, or news articles.[48] With the advent of social media a generation of newborn curators began sharing with the world their favorite media links, images, videos, or memes. For some it became not only a livelihood, but also a source of fame and influence.

In his twenties Matt Drudge worked in a series of convenience and gift stores until his father bought him a computer to help him get his career on track. Drudge started sending out emails with news links to a handful of his friends. His subscribers blossomed and he launched a website, Drudge Report. Drudge rapidly grew attention through scoops from his network of contacts, being the first to report on what would become the Monica Lewinsky scandal, but people mainly came to his site for his links to mainstream news sites, often accompanied by brief, excoriating comments.

While more recently people's media habits have shifted, as recently as 2014 Drudge Report was the single largest source of web traffic to the likes of CNN, Fox News, the *New York Times*, *USA Today*, and the *Wall Street Journal*, far ahead of Facebook or Twitter. Readers didn't go directly to the news sites to browse; they trusted Drudge's selection of news articles to point them to what they should read. Drudge was an early leader in the burgeoning world of content curation, unleashed by the advent of the internet.

To thrive on overload, it is not essential to be a content curator, but it can be enormously helpful. As you uncover the information and ideas that help you achieve your personal objectives, all it takes is sharing from among the content you encounter what you think might be useful to others.

One reason to do so is as a contribution to others. In my 2002 book *Living Networks* I lauded those who were "bringing the networks to life" by connecting ideas and people, contributing to communities, and helping us be collectively more intelligent by surfacing worthwhile content for others.[49] If you have discovered something useful to you, it will undoubtedly be useful to others.

I also noted, "If you help bring the networks to life . . . you will create success for yourself."[50] By donating your insight to the world with minimal effort, you can also bring substantive benefits to yourself, many of which will directly support your purpose and expertise development.

Consistently sharing useful information and insights can bring you immense benefits.

There are four primary outcomes of sharing insights from your quotidian information explorations:

1. **Hone your filtering skills.** The most important reason to curate publicly is to improve your skills at filtering. To select relevant content, you need to be clear on your area

of expertise or interest and have begun to build your own frameworks to make sense of the space. These will help you determine what is truly interesting to your specific audience. Moreover, the challenge of having followers makes you consider more deeply whether content is insightful and its import.

2. **Demonstrate expertise.** As you intelligently parse information, your rapidly developing expertise will have immediate application to your work. Your peers will see the depth of your knowledge, creating trust and helping them consider you an authority.

3. **Boost visibility.** For your expertise to have the greatest impact it needs to be seen and recognized. Those who share insights along their ongoing learning journeys become far more visible in their areas of knowledge, known and readily able to be found.

4. **Build relationships.** The leading experts in almost any given field, those who are pushing the boundaries and not relying on past knowledge, learn alongside a group of peers. Disproportionately, those who are in the vanguard share freely and are open to input and ideas from all sides. Tracking and sharing their insights can not only ratchet up your own understanding, but also build valuable relationships.

There are of course costs to sharing your insights with others as you develop your frameworks and mental models, primarily of time and focus. While the time required for sharing content is not high, if you share on social channels, it is also worth interacting with those who engage with your content. That often has value in itself, but it does take a finite investment of time. Another important factor is that it can divert you from your current attention mode, so where possible bookmark what you find for later sharing.

Inbound Filtering

Judiciously selecting a balanced portfolio of portals and sources lets us maximize the valuable signal from a world of noise. It gives us choice and versatility in how we access information, offering us a daily diet that can nourish without overwhelming us.

At the same time as we discern what is worth pulling toward us, the world is pushing information and demands for our attention at us at a fiendish rate. All while we venture forth seeking what is precious, we are being bombarded with messages of dubious value. To prosper we need to filter these messages efficiently and effectively, leaving our minds as unencumbered as possible.

Some basic principles always apply, including blocking ads, consistently unsubscribing from all but the most valuable emails, guiding your colleagues to communicate on your preferred collaboration platforms, and where possible using human or AI filters to prioritize messages. However, the real nub of the issue is setting explicit rules on what merits your attention.

Your Rules for Saying Yes

Yes is the most powerful word in the English language. It can open up immense new possibilities. But if you say yes to everything you will inevitably be overwhelmed, and not able to seize the most compelling opportunities. So, in fact to truly say yes to the right possibilities, you have to say no far more than you say yes. Establishing specific rules minimizes time and effort; they clearly indicate what merits a positive response.

Everyone is deluged with requests, especially those whose success has made them visible to others. Almost all requests you will receive are for one of three things: your time, your money, or your relationships.

Most people get requests for their time, whether it is to take a real-world or virtual meeting; to look at a website, article, app, or book; or to speak or do an interview. Others ask for access to your relationships, either introductions to people you know or by sharing on social media what they want to promote.

How tightly you define your filtering rules will depend on how deluged you are with inbound requests. Anyone working in venture capital will inevitably be swamped with messages from startup founders. Professional investors set and often publish precise criteria to merit even a second glance at a proposal, which swiftly winnows the deluge.

If you provide contact information on the internet, clearly describe your guidelines for getting a response. Cal Newport, author of *Deep Work* and more recently *A World Without Email*, calls these "sender filters" that reverse the burden of responsibility, asking those sending you messages to first assess whether these meet your filtering criteria, and set expectations for whether or what kind of reply they may receive.[51]

Tim Urban of the blog *Wait But Why* describes what to expect for the different kinds of messages he receives, noting that "you may or may not hear back from us, depending on a lot of things." On author and podcaster Tim Ferriss's website he gives clear instructions on everything he will not respond to, and how you can engage with him.

A central element of your inbound filtering process is defining your potential responses. Only unmitigated enthusiasm should yield a yes; don't commit yourself if you feel half-hearted. If there isn't enough information to make a decision, communicate clearly what you need. Create templates of gracious responses explaining your existing commitments. And don't feel you need to respond to thoughtless messages.

Applying the Power of Filtering

Sensory filtering is one of our brain's fundamental functions; however, its default propensities are often unhelpful in today's information environment. We need to be conscious in our filtering and train ourselves to consistently assess content quality and relevance. Draw on the powers of purpose and framing you have developed to better discern what serves you and what doesn't. Your information intentions will guide you in selecting the portfolios of portals, information sources, and media formats that best suit your objectives.

The power of filtering flows directly into the power of attention. As you will discover in the next chapter, filtering is central to two of the basic attention modes. You will learn how to apply your power of filtering to develop empowering information routines, carefully allocating your time and attention to the activities that will best enable you to thrive.

EXERCISES

Content Filtering Framework

Try consistently applying the framework shown in Figure 3.1 earlier in this chapter as you scan and assess your information sources for one day. Which of the questions are most useful? Which come most into play? How will this change your information habits?

Selecting Information Portals

What information portals will you prioritize? For each portal indicate the approximate proportion of your attention you will allocate and within each your primary sources or tools.

Portal	Proportion of Your Attention (%)	Primary Sources
Direct to media		
Individuals		
Feeds		
Media aggregators		
Social media		

Personal Information Networks

In which domains of expertise should you develop high-value personal information networks?

What action will you take to build them?

Filtering Inbound Requests

What filtering rules will merit a yes to inbound requests?

CHAPTER 4

THE POWER OF ATTENTION

Allocate Awareness with Intention

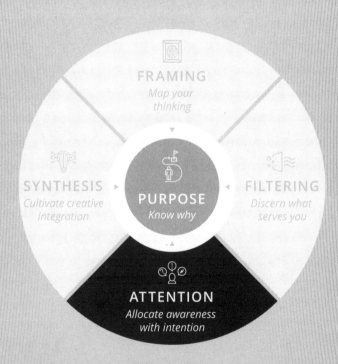

At the end of your life, looking back, whatever
compelled your attention from moment to moment
is simply what your life will have been.[1]

—Oliver Burkeman, author of *Four Thousand Weeks*

Your attention is your most precious gift, but it is a finite resource and constantly being pulled away from you by today's perpetual distractions. Humans cannot truly multitask; the steep cost of switching between tasks means the longer we can remain in a single attention mode at a time, the more effective we will be.

Attention is not one thing; there are six different attention modes that we need to understand and use judiciously to maximize our minds and capabilities: Scanning, Seeking, Assimilating, Deep-diving, Exploring, and Regenerating.

Establishing enabling information routines that set time-boxes for your attention modes will maximize your productivity and outcomes. Just as we can fortify our body through consistent training, we can strengthen our attention with concerted exercise.

On June 9, 2008, Steve Jobs, standing in his signature black turtleneck and jeans in front of an enthusiastic crowd at Apple's annual Worldwide Developer Conference, announced the iPhone 3G. It featured (at the time) superfast 3G access, location services, the freshly launched App Store with a wealth of third-party applications, and to boot, an affordable entry price of $199. This was the true dawn of the smartphone era, drawing in what would be before long the majority of the population to constant information access throughout their waking hours, with a continuous welter of penetrating notifications drawing people back to their devices.

More recently, 47 percent of Americans (no doubt accurately) considered themselves addicted to their cell phones, while 70 percent check their phones within five minutes of receiving a notification.[2] Not surprisingly this behavior tends to fragment our attention, as we are exposed not only to constant interruptions, but also the ever-so-sweet temptation of instant diversion with friends' and celebrities' updates.

Goal Interference

Humans are distinguished from all other animals by their highly evolved goal-setting abilities. We must be in awe at what humans can achieve when they set their minds to it. However, on our paths to our desires we all experience what is called "goal interference," not least from the infinite distractions that can lead us astray.

Unfortunately, "our cognitive control abilities that are necessary for the enactment of our goals . . . do not differ greatly from those observed in other primates, with whom we shared common ancestors tens of millions of years ago," write neuroscientists Adam Gazzaley and psychologist Larry Rosen in *The Distracted Mind*.

The reality is that our cognitive control is highly limited. Our brains are not designed to do what we want in today's saturated information environment. Gazzaley and Rosen believe that "this conflict is escalating into a full-scale war, as modern technological advancements worsen goal interference." The bounteous distractions in our environment are, not surprisingly, massively impeding our ability to achieve our objectives.

The Cost of Task-Switching

Do you think you are good at multitasking? If so, you're wrong. Recent advances in neuroscience have allowed us to observe brain activity while we are engaged in multiple tasks. They verify that humans simply do not have the ability to engage in multiple activities simultaneously. When we think we are multitasking, our brains are in fact rapidly switching between tasks. This entails a high cognitive overhead, so the more you divide your attention, the lower your performance. In fact, those who consider themselves to be good at multitasking consistently perform worse on concurrent tasks than those who don't usually attempt to do this.[3]

The steep cognitive price of task-switching means that to process information efficiently we must keep to single tasks for extended periods. This doesn't mean that we need to be automatons, never distracted by what is around us. Many tasks, such as watching entertainment, cooking, browsing magazines, or walking down the street, do not require our undivided attention. Yet to achieve anything of note we need focus, spending stretches of time in consistent types of attention before moving on to the next task.

The Six Attention Modes

Our brain has many different states, depending on the context. Our neurological patterns will vary dramatically depending on whether we are watching a film, studying for an exam, browsing social media, having a shower, or each of a host of other activities.

We can't—and don't want to—sustain any of these states of mind for excessive periods. Each has its place in enabling us to create the lives we want. The trick is in choosing when we can most usefully apply each frame to our information odysseys.

> ***How you allocate your attention is***
> ***a defining choice in your life.***

Many writers imply that focus is a singular state, in that we are either focused or not. In fact, there is a wide range of mental states and each offers a different locus and breadth of attention.

There are six distinct activities that play a critical part in our ability to thrive on overload. Each one is associated with an attention mode that optimizes our information usage, as shown in Figure 4.1. The diagram depicts each information activity and its quintessence, along with a brief description.

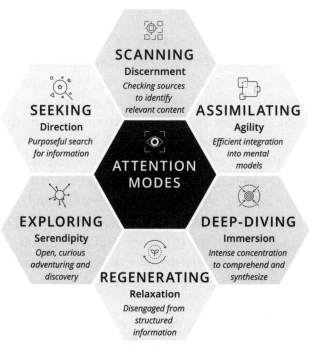

FIGURE 4.1 The Six Attention Modes

Each of the attention modes has an important role to play in our daily immersion in information. The critical issue is in the balance between them, ensuring that each one is used when appropriate. Throughout each day, we need to allocate our attention with clear intention.

Blocks of Attention

As we have seen, there is a dramatic mental cost to switching between attention modes. Reducing the frequency of switching between modes is one of the most important drivers of information mastery. Every distraction and transition detracts from the value of our current activity.

The longer you remain in a single attention mode at a time, the more effective you will be.

The greatest value comes when we deliberately allocate time for each of the attention modes and stick to that activity for that period. If while we are Deep-diving an idea comes up, we should make a note so we can forget it and come back to it later. If we are Exploring and identify a valuable resource, it is often better to park it for time allotted to Assimilating. If you are Seeking specific information and stumble across a fascinating list of tangents, bookmark it for when you are Exploring. Creating structure in your information immersion will pay enormous dividends.

To become true information masters, we need to build routines that allow us to keep on top of change while also leading balanced, happy lives. We can do that by allocating in our daily schedules time to engage in each of the attention modes in ways that support our purpose and goals.

Later in this chapter we will explore how to develop an information routine that empowers you each and every day. Before that let us examine the six attention modes in the rough order many of us use them: Scanning, Seeking, Assimilating, Deep-diving, Exploring, and Regenerating.

Scanning

Every day, every hour, every minute a bounty of new information is generated that might be not just relevant to you, but vital. If you work in any domain that moves faster than a slug's pace, you need to scan broadly and consistently to ensure that you are aware of what is important.

The mechanics of *what* to scan was covered in Chapter 3, in selecting a portfolio of information portals and sources to keep you well informed. The most important part of filtering is establishing the structures that expose you to useful and correct information. In this chapter, scanning addresses *when* you survey the world to uncover what matters, and the state of mind to do this effectively.

Discernment is the defining characteristic of effective scanning, in deciding whether you will skim over something or take a closer look. Given the profusion of information, skimming through our sources must be a highly accelerated process, involving a continuous flow of rapid-fire decisions. Our minds need to be nimble, happier to skip ahead than get bogged down. As such, goal-oriented scanning is often best done when alert.

Efficient Scanning

In a fast-moving world you need to scan for updates regularly. The mistake many make is doing this consistently through the day. If you are a stockbroker or a journalist, you need constant updates to respond to market movements or report on a breaking story. Most of us don't need to be so close to the edge of change.

Often the single behavior shift that can most improve your information habits is checking for news updates less frequently.

Our deep human propensity for novelty can make it hard not to be always looking for the latest. If we can bring ourselves to cordon off most of our scanning activities to specific, limited periods, we can garner substantial benefits. The task is being as effective as possible in your regular checking of sources. Here are a few useful rules:

Stick to your chosen portals and sources. Scanning is a delineated activity; aim to do it efficiently. If after you have done your scheduled review you want to fit in some Exploring, that's fine, but start and finish your defined scan first. As you assess the quality of your feeds or uncover other interesting sources, delete or add to your list of sources you check regularly.

Assess headlines first. This has become much harder as internet headline writers are taught to tease but not disclose the article's point. This comes back to selecting the information sources you will use regularly. If they require you to click through the headline to find out what the article is about, it is an inefficient source and you should likely switch to sources that provide a clearer indication of article content in their titles.

Bookmark for later reading. Scanning is about quickly and efficiently going through your core sources and identifying the content that is worth spending time on. Don't get bogged down in reading articles that require time and dedicated attention; set these aside for when you have the right frame of mind for Assimilation, and complete your Scanning process.

Constrain your scanning time. Assimilating valuable information is more important than Scanning and should take more of your time. If you are spending all your time looking for what's interesting without delving into the detail you will never build depth.

Seeking

The creation of modern search engines was arguably almost as important as the invention of the internet. Now when we want to know something, we only need ask.

While web search is our usual mode of Seeking, we should also consider other approaches. As you have learned, people are often your best resource in finding the information you need. We should not forget that there are libraries full of marvelous books that are not available in digital form. Yet their catalogs are almost always available digitally, allowing us to search for and uncover these gems, potentially followed by a library visit for a Deep-diving session to mine their insights.

As with every focus mode, carve out a period for your stint of Seeking and park for later those resources that merit more attention. Seeking can very easily end up as an Exploring session, leading you to places that may be enthralling but not serve your objective, so as with all attention modes, keep focused! While you are Seeking, follow these principles:

Be clear what you want. The fundamental mental frame for Seeking is direction. Without clarity you risk wandering aimlessly amid the myriad enticing tidbits you will encounter. Having a specific idea of what will be useful to you makes it easy to assess the relevance of what you find.

Scan broadly. The first step is to find as many resources as possible that are relevant to your search. Depending on what you're looking for, don't limit yourself to your usual search engine. Use different search engines, and when appropriate use academic search engines such as Google Scholar, Microsoft Academic, or ResearchGate. I use an initial set of search terms and open tabs to all of the pages that seem potentially useful, based on their title and the meta text in the search engine. I then try to identify alternative search terms, since authors and publishers could use different words from the ones I start with, until I have uncovered the most promising starting points.

Delve deep. For some information quests you need to go beyond the surface. When entrepreneur Martine Rothblatt was striving to identify a cure for her daughter's disease, she adapted a technique called "shepardizing" she had learned in her legal studies. The name comes from Shepard's Citations, which tracks every mention of a legal case or statute. For every promising medical paper Rothblatt found, she went to its citations, and in turn to their citations, creating a spiderweb to reach the vast majority of pertinent published content.[4] The process is deeply time-consuming but enables thorough discovery of the most relevant sources. The treatment Rothblatt uncovered not only saved her daughter's life, but also provided the foundation for her company United Therapeutics, which has since been valued at over $9 billion.

Narrow swiftly for later assimilation. Go through all of the resources you have uncovered, quickly winnowing. If you have opened multiple relevant tabs, quickly scan through each to see whether they may have valuable information. If they are sufficiently promising, bookmark them for later Assimilating or Deep-diving sessions. If there are only one or two points of interest, note the ideas and move on. Be efficient at assessing the potential value of content so you can allocate dedicated attention to what is worth absorbing.

Once we have found intriguing content through Scanning and Seeking, we need to integrate it into our thinking. This requires a shift of gears; Assimilating is a distinct state of mind.

Assimilating

Two years into his stint as junior senator of Massachusetts, an ambitious John F. Kennedy took the time to drive with his brother Bobby one hour each way to attend a weekly evening course at Johns Hopkins University titled How to Read Better and Faster.[5] Later President Kennedy claimed to read 1,200 words per minute (he was also reputed to hold a world record for talking speed, peaking at 327 words per minute in one of his speeches). He invited speed-reading entrepreneur Evelyn Wood to the White House to teach his staff, with Richard Nixon following suit and Jimmy Carter also taking the Evelyn Wood course.[6]

Even for those of us who do not have the demands of being president of the United States, speed-reading is a tantalizing concept, promising the ability to absorb content far faster than the usual rate of 200 to 400 words per minute. Yet the issue is not so much how fast you read, but how much you take in. Assimilating means integrating ideas into your thinking, truly absorbing and comprehending them. Better assimilation is not necessarily faster. You need to intelligently adjust your pace so that you can engage fully with the most worthwhile ideas, to make them yours.

Switching Gears

A race car driver will put her vehicle in top gear for straight and predictable stretches of track, then downshift as she reaches the curves that require precise attention and control. In the same way, as we read we should be ready to switch gears between racing through less relevant ideas and slowing dramatically where we want to fully understand the content.

Uncovering interesting content or information has only limited value by itself. You need to take the content and ideas and integrate them into your frameworks and mental models. Allocate specific time for Assimilation, rather than trying to fit it in whenever you stumble across an article or resource that you want to absorb. This can be whenever suits—for example, while eating, commuting, or exercising. Nir Eyal and Marina Gorbis both absorb much of the content they have previously selected through audio while working out at the gym.[7]

The quintessence of Assimilating is agility. You have identified content that you have decided is worth your attention. But you don't yet know how much value there is in the content you are delving into. You have to be nimble to extract value as efficiently as possible.

How to Comprehend Faster

What superpower would you choose? Flight? Telepathy? Laser eyes? When Bill Gates was asked this question, his simple reply was, "Being able to read super-fast."[8] You can make substantial progress toward that aspiration by following (and practicing) these four principles:

1. **Hone visual reading skills.** We can process faster visually than through any other sense. It is critical to eliminate any subvocalization while we read. Taking in larger chunks of text at a time by expanding your field of vision is a critical component of effective reading.

2. **Minimize fixations.** We process visually through what are called saccades, in which our eyes fix on one place, then move to the next. When reading, our objective is to increase how much text we can absorb in each fixation. Developing this skill takes work but pays off in spades. You want where possible to take in a whole line or group of lines in one saccade, not moving your eyes from left to right. To make this easier, where possible reduce line

width: if using a tablet, read in portrait rather than landscape mode; on computers reduce the width of the browser window.

3. **Make sense of the whole.** When you are reading to extract value you should rarely start at the beginning and go to the end. The opening sections of a book or long article will hopefully neatly summarize the content, while the end may provide a recap or conclusion. For some kinds of books, I find it useful to start by skimming the entire text in 15 minutes or so to get a sense of the overall structure and argument and to identify the sections that I expect to find most interesting.

4. **Guide your pace.** The reading habit that slows us the most is regression, going back to look at what we have already read. To get into the habit of a consistent pace, move your finger or a pencil steadily down the page to guide your eyes. When Assimilating, we should vary pace according to content. If you are already familiar with the ideas in the text, you can speed up; if you encounter interesting concepts, slow down to absorb them.

Observing these simple principles can immediately and significantly accelerate your pace of text comprehension. If you'd like to go deeper into improving your reading, check out the Resources for Thriving at the end of this book.

Note-Taking and Framing

The function of Assimilating is integrating ideas into your frameworks and mental models. In Chapter 2 we discussed the immense value of taking notes, and the value of making them in connected note-taking systems that link concepts to other references.

Taking notes not only allows you to capture any specific insights you gain and readily find content again. The very act of writing a note also helps you make sense of an idea and impress it on your mind. Many people who read material end up unchanged aside from a vague recollection of what they went through. Anyone who makes a note when reading is effectively integrating the content into their mental models.

> *Making notes is more than absorbing ideas;*
> *it is the process of making them yours.*

As Edgar Allan Poe put it, "Marking a book is literally an experience of your differences or agreements with the author. It is the highest respect you can pay him."

Deep-Diving

Our minds wander. This is not just from time to time; it is almost constant, leading scientists to describe this as the "default mode" of our brains.[9] We spend most of our waking hours at the surface. Sometimes we need the intent and will to dive deep. Arguably the biggest division among us is between those willing and able to immerse themselves in ideas and thinking for extended periods, and the majority who perennially skim across the superficial.

In the state of Deep-diving we can absorb content for true comprehension, deliberately discern patterns, identify new connections, and refine the structure of our frameworks. This is a time for purposeful sense-making, exploring perspectives, and laying the groundwork for effective decisions.

"As the competitive and technological landscape continues to shift at an accelerating rate you will require more time than ever before to just think," says Jeff Weiner, executive chairman of LinkedIn. "That thinking, if done properly, requires uninterrupted focus; thoroughly developing and questioning assumptions; synthesizing all of the data, information and knowledge that's incessantly coming your way; connecting dots, bouncing ideas off of trusted colleagues; and iterating through multiple scenarios. In other words, it takes time."[10]

Indeed, there are two foundations to Deep-diving: allocating sufficient blocks of time and accessing the right frame of mind. Deep-diving is several levels more intense than most information engagement; it is a distinct state. Some, such as software developers, writers, or researchers, may need to get into this state every day. However, everyone who wants to thrive in our world needs to carve out regular times to dive into the depths of forming useful mental models.

We should treat this as a distinct, special state. In other focus modes you might choose to keep yourself open to important notifications. Deep-diving is a state of total immersion. There are four critical steps to being able to dive deep:

1. **Carve out sufficient blocks of time.** It takes your mind a while to get focused. Few can switch on instantaneously. The minimum time for a deep-dive session should be an hour; many recommend aiming for three hours or so. Consider the best time of day for you to be hyperfocused based on your daily cycles. It also depends on your circumstances: for example, whether you have children to get to school, or your typical workday is so fragmented that you can't carve out extended periods during normal working hours.

2. **Design your environment.** Create a space in which you can be completely comfortable for an extended period. Be sure the ergonomics are good, with a chair in which you can sit with a straight back or at a standing desk, with your screen close to eye height. Avoid using a laptop without an external screen, as you have to bend your neck to look down. Set up lighting that is comfortable.

3. **Eliminate all interruptions.** In Deep-diving you eliminate all distractions. Close your email; turn off phones and all

social media notifications. A variety of apps such as Cold Turkey or Freedom allow you to shut off all applications and notifications for the period of your choice. If you're writing, distraction-free writing apps like FocusWriter support complete focus. Block out the time in your calendar so colleagues can see you're busy, and make sure anyone in your office or household knows that you should be interrupted only for something highly urgent.

4. **Refresh with regular breaks.** We cannot sustain focused attention for extended periods; you need to rest your mind periodically. The basic rest-activity cycle (BRAC) theory states that we go through regular cycles of alertness and relaxation lasting around 90 minutes. Others suggest shorter focus times: for example, in the Pomodoro technique you work for 25-minute stints with 5-minute breaks. See what works best for you. What is critical is substantially changing your state and activity during your breaks. Be sure to stand up, walk around, look outside, perhaps do some breathing exercises. Don't browse news or social media on the same device you're using for your work—that won't refresh you.

Soundtracks for Deep-Diving

When Michael Lewis is preparing to write his books, which have included *Moneyball, The Big Short,* and many other bestsellers, he carefully compiles the soundtrack for the project. He takes suggestions from his wife and children, building a wide variety of upbeat tracks that he then plays relentlessly on repeat throughout his book writing.

He writes with his headphones on so he can't hear anything going on around him. "It's a device for shutting out other interruption and for creating kind of an emotion, a feeling," Lewis says. Because he has heard each track hundreds of times, it ceases to register mentally. "I'm just in my own space and I kind of cease to hear the sound."[11]

Futurist and author Amy Webb is an aficionado of brown noise, random noise mainly in the lower spectrum, which can sound like the surf or wind. "Because I'm more sensitive to higher frequencies, brown noise helps me focus intensively. It's amazing how well it works," Webb reports.[12]

When we are Deep-diving, soundtracks can help us to focus and drown out sounds around us. Some people prefer silence, but this requires a workplace away from any disturbances, a luxury not available to everyone. Comfortable noise-canceling headphones playing the right soundscape can create an oasis for undisturbed thinking, even in busy environments.

Some companies profess to have created music that specifically helps you focus. You should experiment and find what works best for you. Music is not just to drown out background noise, but also to create a positive mood; it can help you not just focus but also enjoy your Deep-diving sessions.

Exploring

Humans are intrinsically explorers. It is not just pleasurable to meander through the back alleys of the web and beyond; it can also be extremely valuable as we stumble upon insights or perspectives that we would never have found if we were overly focused. Rather than demonize "surfing," we should understand it as an invaluable element of our information routine. To make our far-flung reconnoitering useful we need to shift our attention from tight focus to the peripheries.

There is a reason that houses with expansive views, from hilltops or looking out over the ocean or a lake, attract premium prices. There is something uniquely attractive—and beneficial—about being exposed to broad vistas. Andrew Huberman, professor of neurobiology at Stanford University, says that when we go into panoramic vision—for example, by seeing horizons or walking down the street—it has a calming effect on our nervous system and disengages our vigilance of attention, the tight visual focus that we usually have, for example, when we look at screens or are indoors.[13]

You can readily practice peripheral vision. Stop reading, look straight ahead, and see what you can notice at the edges of your field of sight. Try gently redirecting your visual attention to the edges of what you can see, without moving your eyes. You will likely find yourself calmer and more relaxed. This simple activity puts you in a state of mind similar to meditation. As you walk around during the day try deliberately entering panoramic vision, directing your attention beyond what is in front of your eyes.

Broader visual perception, perhaps not surprisingly, can expand our conceptual understanding. Studies have shown that people who broadened their visual field were more likely to experience insight in solving problems.[14] See more broadly, and you will think more broadly. The ability to expand your visual perception also enables faster reading by minimizing fixations and allowing you to more readily absorb concepts.

Enhancing Serendipity

Serendipity was once voted by Britons as their favorite word and is said by interpreters to be one of the English words most difficult to translate.[15] Meaning the faculty of making happy and unexpected discoveries, it comes from the enchanting tale of *The Three Princes of Serendip* (the ancient name for Sri Lanka), a fairy tale in which the eponymous three princes enable felicitous connections, not by pure accident but by actively creating the conditions for them to happen.[16]

The point about the origin story of the word is that serendipity is often not fortuitous; you can behave in ways that make it more likely to occur. Here are a few practices that can make it more likely that you experience fortune in your unfettered information adventures:

> **Take the path less traveled.** "Two roads diverged in a wood, and I—I took the one less traveled by, and that has made all the difference," wrote poet Robert Frost. As we turn off the

information highways into beguiling byways, in Exploration mode we can give ourselves permission to go, not necessarily where fewer people wander, but certainly where we usually don't go.

Keep following your fascination. In exploration mode you can follow the intriguing link that you might pass over when you're in a more focused state. If you find something interesting, keep following it down the rabbit hole, or use it as inspiration for another starting point. Keep moving unless you find gold. The more diversions you take, the more likely you will uncover inspiration.

Search in different places. If you're used to searching in a search engine or YouTube, try podcasts, Twitter, Pinterest, academic search platforms, foreign language search engines, or your books, if you keep them digitally. Investor Sanjay Bakshi regularly seeks ideas in his own book collection, saying, "You sometimes discover things that you didn't know existed—the serendipitous discovery of wonderful words of wisdom about a certain topic in your Kindle library is amazing, and when that happens, I have my eureka moments."[17]

Start with an intriguing person or word. Sometimes I search on nonmainstream platforms using a word or unusual combination of words that might lead to something interesting yet surprising. Words I have used include (of course) "serendipity" as well as combinations of terms germane to my research. A valuable and often fun exercise is to select an intriguing person who evidently thinks differently from you as a starting point for exploration.

Cultivate your faculty for serendipity. Learn by giving yourself feedback. When you are exploring, register mentally when you encounter something surprisingly interesting or useful. How did you find it? What might you do to make this kind of discovery more likely to happen again?

Regenerating

Stephen and Rachel Kaplan met when studying at Oberlin College, an Ohio liberal arts institution, swiftly recognized themselves as soul mates, and were married at the ages of 21 and 20, respectively. They went on to complete their doctorates in psychology at the University of Michigan at the same time and spent the remainder of their careers working and collaborating, both becoming full professors at the Ann Arbor university.

In the first decade of their careers the Kaplans focused primarily on traditional psychology research topics such as memory and arousal, until the USDA Forest Service engaged them to study the benefits of a wilderness challenge program. Stephen described the results as "incredibly impressive," sparking a transformation in their lives to focus on the value of nature for human cognition.[18]

The Kaplans proposed that there are two types of attention: directed attention and fascination. Overuse of directed attention, which is what we primarily apply in our everyday world of information immersion, is not sustainable, leading to "directed attention fatigue."[19] Being in nature draws our attention, not in a highly directed fashion, but in fascination with the infinite variations and beauty in any natural environment. Subsequent research led to the development of attention restoration theory, which focuses on how different environments, particularly natural, help our limited attention capabilities to regenerate.

Stephen later drew a distinction between "soft fascination" and "hard fascination."[20] The fascination you feel in nature is gentle, allowing other thoughts to emerge and flow as you contemplate your environment. Other types of fascination, such as watching movies or sports events, absorb your attention and prevent thinking about other things.

"Another day of staring at the big screen while scrolling through my little screen so as to reward myself for staring at the medium screen all week." This widely shared tweet by journalist Delia Cai incisively captured the zeitgeist during the height of the pandemic in 2020. The many who turn to watching streaming video to recover from their hard work in front of the computer may be relaxing, but they are not regenerating their attention and ability to focus.

Intensely focused attention is not sustainable, nor should we want that. It is critical to recognize that as we shift between different modes of focus, regeneration is one of the most essential. Taking time away from intensity and immersion is in fact vital to being able to sustain our more engaged styles of focus. Every day we need to switch off entirely from information and digital engagement to regenerate.

Going for a stroll in nature, exercising, having a bath, reading fiction, carefully cooking a meal, meditating, lying on a couch daydreaming, playing an instrument, and extended sensual explorations with a partner are all ways that I and many others regenerate, taking us away from the aggressive submersion in information that is intrinsic to modern life. What are the activities that work best for you to regenerate yourself? If you wish to be as productive and effective as possible, these must be part of your daily schedule.

In fact, these kinds of activities put you in a state of mind that is highly conducive to synthesis and insight, when your very best ideas come to you. Constant busyness will let you achieve tasks, but it is when you pull back to see the big picture that you will identify opportunities and recognize where best to apply your efforts.

The Value of Information Routines

Most people begin their day by checking their emails and the news, "so I know the world didn't break when I was asleep," as Seth Godin put it,[21] but don't take that as an assumption on how you should work. We usually want to find out what's going on in the world, but other than quickly confirming that the world is still intact, we can do this whenever best suits us.

Daniel Ek, founder and CEO of music-streaming giant Spotify, moves to the beat of his own drum. He says, "I wake up at around 6:30 in the morning and spend some time with my kids and wife. At 7:30, I go work out. At 8:30, I go for a walk—even in the winter. I've found this is often where I do my best thinking. At 9:30, I read for thirty minutes to an hour. Sometimes I read the news, but you'll also find an ever-rotating stack of books in my office, next to my bed, on tables around the house. Books on history, leadership, biographies. It's a pretty eclectic mix—much like my taste in music. Finally, my 'work' day really starts at 10:30."[22]

Most of us tend to fairly consistent morning information activities. Fewer establish deliberate daily patterns for allocating their precious attention. Establishing methodical information habits is a huge opportunity.

> *Following thoughtfully designed information routines will dramatically enhance your effectiveness.*

Planning when and for how long you engage in specific attention modes minimizes costly task-switching and ensures you are allocating time to the most valuable activities. The routines that will work best are unique to each of us; we need to discover them by trying.

Optimizing for Your Chronotype

One of the beguiling things about humans is that we are all different. Our states of mind and neurochemical balances consistently shift through the day, each with our own distinctive patterns. Knowing yourself well enough to select the best times of day for different activities is a superpower that can massively enhance your productivity and effectiveness.

Do you consider yourself to be a "morning person" or an "evening person"? Academics call this our chronotype, creating measures of what they describe as the "morningness" or "evening-ness" of a person.[23]

One important implication is the best time for your Deep-diving sessions, which are far more likely to be productive if timed to coincide with your greatest cognitive capacity. Because of the basic rest-activity cycle and its differences between individuals, we also need to be aware of how our alertness varies through the day. Some people experience a slump after lunch or other meals, which can be diet-related, but which should shape how you allocate your time (and perhaps what you choose to eat).

Timeboxing Your Information Engagement

Business used to be slow, predictable, and comfortable (well, at least compared to today!). As the pace of change accelerated, software development began to shift from traditional project man-agement techniques to a set of methodologies commonly called "agile," allowing far faster development of usable software and improved responsiveness to changing requirements. One of the principles that supported agile development was "timeboxing," which simply allocates a fixed period of time to work on a deliv-erable. This meant that if the planned functionality couldn't be achieved in the time allocated, the scope was adjusted to include only the most important elements, forcing prioritization of features and work.

In 2004, blogger and author Steve Pavlina wrote a post mod-estly titled "Timeboxing."[24] He described how he had been inspired to apply the concept from software development to his personal time management. Pavlina concluded by writing that his wife had come home with dinner and a movie rental so that was the end of the post.

The idea of timeboxing for personal scheduling has gained sub-stantial traction in recent years. Ardent advocates include both Bill Gates and Elon Musk, who divide their working days into seg-ments dedicated to specific activities, not allowing them to bleed into successive timeboxes.

Nir Eyal, author of *Indistractable*, calls timeboxing "the nearest thing we have to productivity magic."[25] If you allocate time to working on a project, you can hold yourself accountable for whether you did that or were distracted by social media or other things. You can assess whether time you block out for being with your family or out in nature is being cut into by distractions. In exactly the same way, if you want and intend to spend time browsing Instagram or watching streaming shows, you can do that with a clear conscience simply by allocating that time in your calendar.

This is particularly important for those whose jobs mean there are constant demands on their time. LinkedIn's Jeff Weiner blocks out in his calendar the thinking time he needs to do his job well. "In aggregate, I schedule between 90 minutes and two hours of these buffers every day (broken down into 30- to 90-minute blocks)," he shares. "It's a system I developed over the last several years in response to a schedule that was becoming so jammed with back-to-back meetings that I had little time left to process what was going on around me or just think."[26]

Billionaire PayPal cofounder Max Levchin reports, "I tend to come up with precise routines and repeat them obsessively every day. In perfect detail, every morning at home looks the same. By cutting out the contemplation of what to do next, I achieve extreme efficiencies."[27]

Considerations in Setting Your Information Routine

You are unique, in ways that you understand and some that you have yet to discover. Generic prescriptions aren't useful. You need to work out, to some extent by trial and error, what schedules for your attention modes will work best for you. As you develop your information routines, take into account these principles:

Don't necessarily start the day with information. A staggering 80 percent of people say they check their smartphones within 10 minutes of waking.[28] Don't do this as a reflex; consider letting your thoughts flow freely for a while, as many highly successful people choose to do. Former Disney CEO Bob Iger says, "I create a firewall with technology, by the way, in that I try to exercise and think before I read. Because if I read, it throws me off, it's distracting. I'm immediately thinking about usually someone else's thoughts instead of my own. I like being alone with my own thoughts, and it gives me an opportunity to not just replenish but to organize, and it's important."[29]

Concentrate Scanning time. Many people begin the day wanting to find out if there was any major news overnight. This can be done by Scanning the headlines in a few minutes, though many people take the time to get their full "news fix" at this time. Unless you need continuous updates for your work, consider my precept of limiting update frequency. Do you really need to scan news headlines multiple times during the day?

Find time pockets for Assimilating. A key choice is whether you assimilate your articles when you find them, or park them to read later. Brian Stelter, the media correspondent of CNN and formerly the *New York Times*, reports that, "between 7 a.m. and 9 a.m., I start opening what ends up being dozens of browser tabs—links from Twitter, links from Facebook, stories in *The Times*, stories that Jamie sends—on my computer. My goal is to close all those by the end of the day. . . . I'll at least skim all those open tabs by the end of the day."[30] Make sure that you allocate sufficient time to making sense of the content you have flagged so you can incorporate it into your thinking.

Block out Deep-diving. Deep-diving stands alone; by its nature it requires an extended period of focus. Even if you don't use timeboxing at the center of your time management, be sure to block out time in your calendar for your highly focused sessions. It is the only way you can get sufficient depth, for this limited period shutting everything off and brooking no interruptions.

Use Exploring for fun breaks. Healthy information habits include regularly going beyond your usual sources. If your inclination when you are taking a brief break from highly focused work is to check social media feeds, instead try going on a little adventure to see what you can stumble upon that is both fascinating and different from your usual fare. It will be far more refreshing.

Schedule times for Regenerating. Our attention needs regular regeneration, and watching streaming shows doesn't do the job. If you can, set a time each day for something that helps revitalize your mind, perhaps a walk in nature, playtime with your pet, or completing an adult coloring book. On weekends go on a hike or cycle or join your child on the playground. Do whatever you enjoy the most, knowing it also strongly supports pragmatic achievement.

Beyond Information Addiction

"Dost thou love life?" inquired Benjamin Franklin. "Then do not squander time, for that is the stuff life is made of." Being alive is an incredible gift, offering us beauty in the moment and always incredible potential to work toward worthwhile outcomes. With all that we could do with our time, when we look back on our lives, might we wish we'd spent more time checking our social media feeds?

Many people accurately describe themselves as "news junkies," not able to keep away from their regular fix of the latest updates. Living in a world in which we can instantly slake our craving for the new, most of us often find that temptation irresistible. Our pernicious addiction is exacerbated by almost every aspect of the modern world.

We need to acknowledge we are information addicts. There is no shame in it. This allows us to act on it, to work to control our addiction.

I certainly admit to being an addict, not adequately able to control my craving for the latest in news and my networks. It is built into who we are, so if you are not an information addict, you have singular self-control, well done! But if we admit the reality of it, we can undertake to improve our habits.

The path of Alcoholics Anonymous, helping alcoholics stay sober, is unfortunately not open to information addicts. We cannot forswear our addiction completely and remain part of modern society. We need to be able to engage with information without it becoming compulsive and taking over more of our lives than we wish. These are skills that we can learn, practice, and develop.

Techniques for Freedom and Choice

There are a range of techniques we can use to help us transcend our addiction and keep focused, to help us tend toward enabling information habits rather than ones that sap our time, energy, and life. Use any or all of the techniques in this section as you are inclined to gain control over information:

Minimize notifications. Do you really want to be a slave of a device that interrupts you with what are almost always trivialities? The single easiest and most powerful thing you can do to take control of your life and maintain focus is reduce to a minimum the overt notifications you receive. The first thing I do when I get a new phone or download a new app is switch off sound notifications. Set up your phone so that it only rings or notifies you of a text message if it is from someone you know you will want to answer immediately.

Manage expectations. If you reply immediately to messages, you are setting people up to expect that you will always do that. Scheduling specific times of day for messaging avoids constant task-switching and can substantially increase productivity. If your work requires frequent collaborative exchanges, make sure there are times when you can switch off, if necessary letting your colleagues know you won't be available for those periods.

Become aware of your actions. The first step to transcending the lure of information distractions is to be aware of your actions. Try to notice when you pick up your phone or device. Don't let it be a reflex action: if you find your phone in your hand, ask yourself why. What do you want to achieve? If it is just to check there haven't been any critical messages, then do that and put it down. If it is to relieve your boredom or provide distraction from a challenging task, give yourself alternatives for what you could do instead.

Delay gratification. If you feel an impulse to check your email or social media or the latest news, acknowledge your desire, but tell yourself you will do it in 5 or 10 minutes. This gives you more focus time during which you might transcend your transient desire and exercise your attention muscles. As importantly, it demonstrates that you are not powerless in the face of your addiction; exerting control in this small way builds your capacity for choice over your information desires.

Substitute other activities. The desire for distraction can be sated in many ways. When I take a break from focus work at home, I try to pick up my guitar for a few minutes, do some breathing exercises, go for a brief walk outside, or read an interesting article on my reading list rather than check my phone for updates. Consider what would fulfill your brain's hankering for a break without diving into the bottomless abyss of social media or news updates.

Limit time. If you sometimes want to reward yourself for a stretch of focus time by browsing updates, memes, or political gossip, indulge yourself. Before you start, simply decide how long is reasonable to spend on this before you resume focus work, and set your timer. Wallow and enjoy, then when your time is up switch your frame of mind back to the task at hand.

Get help from apps. Just as technology can lead us astray, it can also help us. There are myriad apps and tools that can assist us to block distractions, maintain focus, and transcend addiction. Have a look at the Resources for Thriving section at the end of the book for a list of tools to help improve your information habits.

Regularly switch off completely. The practice of "digital sabbaths," eschewing technology or least email and social media for a day a week or selected weekends, is highly beneficial, helping reset your brain's overly established patterns.

Strengthening Your Attention

An early study compared how Zen masters and untrained people respond to the world. Researchers used brain wave sensors to measure the subjects' "startle response," which indicates people's reaction to unexpected stimuli.

When a metronome was started next to untrained people, for the first few ticks they showed a strong response that quickly subsided until the ticks of the metronome barely registered. This is completely natural. Our brains are geared to novelty and actively filter out what recurs consistently.

However, when the scientists tested Zen practitioners, they found an intriguing response. Just like the nontrained people, Zen masters were startled by the initial tick of the metronome. Then as the metronome continued ticking, their response remained almost the same as for the first tick, on and on.[31]

The Zen masters were not becoming habituated to repeated sensory impressions. Everything was fresh to them, even if they had experienced it before. They had trained their brain not to filter out the world around them, but to be constantly paying attention.

One of the reasons I moved to Japan in my late twenties was my longstanding fascination with Zen. I ended up living for a year in a Zen dojo while I worked as a financial journalist, meditating twice a day and performing chores for the community before and after my long train commutes to my work in central Tokyo. My Zen master, Nishijima-Sensei, taught me the path of full attention and how it can help us "distinguish the important from the trivial."[32]

A highly distinctive characteristic of Zen meditation is that it is performed with eyes open facing a wall. Zen is not about shutting yourself off from the world. It is about "experiencing reality." Zen practitioners are continually paying attention. If there is a fly buzzing around or disturbances, these are not to be ignored, they are merely noticed. I have found meditation invaluable not just in being able to focus and be more emotionally balanced, but also in heightening my perception of the world around me.

Meditation and Awareness

"Meditation has probably been the single most important reason for whatever success I've had," proclaims Ray Dalio, billionaire founder of leading hedge fund Bridgewater and author of *Principles*.[33] Other endorsements of the value of meditation come from scores of leaders, including the likes of Marc Benioff, founder of Salesforce, Padmasree Warrior, a director of Microsoft and Spotify, and author Yuval Noah Harari, who says, "Without the focus and clarity provided by this practice, I could not have written *Sapiens* and *Homo Deus*," books that have together sold over 20 million copies.[34]

Despite the clear value, it would be fair to say that most people struggle with starting and continuing meditation. Not everyone wants to meditate, and that's fine. However, hopefully what you read here will provide a further small nudge in that direction. I will provide some suggestions on starting meditation, as well as other practices to help control your attention. Any effort you put into it will be amply rewarded.

As author Daniel Goleman notes, "attention works much like a muscle—use it poorly and it can wither; work it well and it grows."[35] If we want to strengthen our body, we go to a gym regularly to exercise. We don't need to kick off with an athlete's regimen; we just get started and gradually build over time. In exactly the same way, if we want to strengthen our focus, we need to start deliberately exerting our attention, even in small ways, and in time make our practice consistent. There is no other way to improve.

There are dozens of different types of meditation. Practitioners of transcendental meditation repeat a mantra given to them by their teacher. Many forms of meditation including Vipassana start with a focus on your breath. Chakra meditators focus on the energy centers in their body. Body scan meditation draws attention to different parts of your body in turn.

What is common to all meditation is consistent attention. It is absolutely inevitable that our minds wander; it is the default condition of our brains. When meditators become aware that their minds are wandering, they gently draw their attention back to their chosen focus. Practice makes them more able to maintain their attention, so they wander less frequently and are more readily able to resume their concentration.

Steve Jobs meditated consistently through his life from age 19. "If you just sit and observe, you will see how restless your mind is," he said. "If you try to calm it, it only makes it worse, but over time it does calm, and when it does, there's room to hear more subtle things—that's when your intuition starts to blossom and you start to see things more clearly and be in the present more. Your mind just slows down, and you see a tremendous expanse in the moment. You see so much more than you could see before."[36]

How to Start to Meditate

If you already meditate consistently, congratulations! You not only understand the benefits, you are taking sustained action that will consistently improve your attentional capabilities. If you don't meditate and have a glimmer of an inclination to try, follow these guidelines:

Begin with very short periods, but try to do it every day. Don't be overambitious. Numerous studies have demonstrated substantial benefits of meditating for short periods, and your initial intent is to build a habit. Even if you feel exceptionally busy, you should be able to find 10 minutes to do something that will almost certainly increase your productivity. If that seems hard, start with five minutes. Only when you feel like it, gradually increase the duration to whatever period suits you. While longer meditation periods will have greater benefits, don't believe anyone who suggests brief meditation sessions aren't valuable.

Focus on your breathing. We all breathe, so it is easy to pay attention to our breathing, as many forms of meditation do. Focus on the in breath and the out breath; just be aware.

Try meditating with your eyes open. It is probably easier to meditate with eyes closed, as most traditions suggest, so do that if it works better for you. Personally, I prefer meditating with eyes open as it emphasizes that I am paying attention to the world, not shutting it off. It also allows me to expand my visual attention while I meditate, as we learned earlier.

Consider it practice in returning to your attention. You will inevitably get distracted and may end early meditation sessions feeling that you never had control of your attention. That is completely OK—it is a journey. Consider it a win when you notice that your mind is wandering and return your attention to your breath. Every time you become aware that your attention has flown the coop and you come back, you have strengthened your attentional muscles, giving you more control.

Set a time of day or cue. Choose an activity or event that will trigger when you meditate—for example, after a morning shower, before making dinner, or during a scheduled morning break. James Clear of *Atomic Habits* fame calls this "habit stacking," making the activity automatic rather than something you need to decide to do.[37]

Enjoy it! It will be hard to meditate consistently if you consider it a chore. When you are paying full attention, with every breath you are living fully, experiencing yourself, your evanescent thoughts, and your environment. Savor the uncommon every-moment awareness. Also appreciate the difference you may feel after you meditate. You might find you start to grow hungry for this state of mind.

Awareness Practices

Whether or not you meditate, you can improve your attention control simply in how you go about your daily pursuits. In their book *Mindfulness*, Oxford University professor Mark Williams and journalist Danny Penman propose what they call "habit breaking," each week choosing one daily ritual such as teeth brushing or taking a shower and each time giving full awareness to the experience.[38] Instead of doing these activities automatically, without thinking, you exercise your attention.

Throughout each day you have opportunities to pay full attention. See what happens when you give absolute and full attention to someone when they are speaking to you. Every time you eat is a possibility to give your attention to the food you are consuming and relish its flavors. Whenever I'm waiting at a pedestrian crossing, I take it as a cue to stop thinking and focus on my breathing and what's around me. These kinds of practices not only increase the richness of your life, but they also develop your ability to pay attention to what you choose, with powerful benefits in an information-saturated world.

Choosing the Power of Attention

The first step to choosing the power of attention is simply understanding that there are different modes that each have their place. Rather than flitting about through the day, strive to engage in consistent attention for extended periods. Enjoy the variety of exploring intriguing back alleys and taking the space to regenerate, as well as immersing in stretches of deeper focus.

Make the effort to consider and set enabling information routines, allocating time judiciously to the activities that benefit you the most. Attention is like a muscle that we can work to strengthen. Select among the many practices you have learned to develop your faculties.

In Chapter 5 we study how to expand our unique human capability of synthesis. This brings together and builds on facets of each of the other four powers, supported by our ability to adopt and move between attention modes.

EXERCISES

Your Information Routine

Record your initial thoughts on developing an enabling schedule for engaging with information. For each attention mode, write intended times of the day for this activity, the duration, and frequency (times per week, daily, or more frequently).

	When?	How Long?	How Frequently?
Scanning			
Seeking			
Assimilating			
Deep-diving			
Exploring			
Regenerating			

What will you do to embed these schedules and practices into your daily activities?

Practices for Strengthening Attention

What will you do to develop your capacity for attention? What practices will you undertake, and when in your daily routine?

CHAPTER 5

THE POWER OF SYNTHESIS

Cultivate Creative Integration

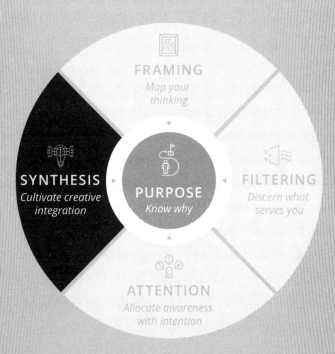

> Comparing the capacity of computers to the capacity of the human brain, I've often wondered, where does our success come from? The answer is synthesis, the ability to combine creativity and calculation, art and science, into a whole that is much greater than the sum of its parts.[1]
>
> **—Garry Kasparov, former World Chess Champion**

In an economy founded on information abundance, the lion's share of value goes to those who can synthesize a multitude of elements to comprehend the whole, build expertise, make better decisions, perceive opportunities, and keep ahead of machines.

To create a wellspring of synthesis we need a foundation of openness to new information, on which we build our capacities to make creative connections and integrate disparate, sometimes paradoxical ideas. These enable us to continuously enrich our mental models to become more complex and useful. Rounding out our capabilities, we can learn to nurture the states of mind in which synthesis is most likely to occur.

The final application of our capacity for synthesis is better decisions. In an exceptionally uncertain world, the best outcomes come from decisions that let us learn, refine our assessment of probabilities, and withstand contrarian thinking.

n our formative years our parents tended to our cognitive development by giving us educational books. You were probably given a join-the-dots figure, in which you connected dots in sequence for a hidden image to emerge on the page. Drawing lines between consecutively numbered dots is fairly easy for a child. As you drew successive lines you tried to work out what the image might depict, until in one moment you finally discerned the pattern being formed.

If you want to experience this with a slightly more advanced example, try joining the dots in Figure 5.1. As you progress, try to discern the pattern, noticing when you recognize the concept portrayed, probably in a single moment.

For adults, "connecting the dots" refers to pulling together a disparate set of information, occurrences, issues, or events to reveal concealed patterns and make sense of what at first blush appears to be unrelated. This is often experienced as an instant of insight and clarity, when the relationships are suddenly obvious and the entire picture comes into focus.

The ultimate reason to engage with information is to understand the world better, and thus learn how best to create what we desire. Knowing many facts is useless. We need to build a lattice of meaningful connections, drawing together what we encounter into a holistic view that enables intensely productive action.

Synthesis is precisely the antithesis of analysis. To perceive the whole, we must necessarily transcend reductionist, overly rational thinking. We need to deliberately cultivate our subtle, often evanescent ability to synthesize today's incredibly complexity by tending to what is below the surface of our minds as much as to our conscious thinking.

Synthesis and Human Progress

Humans are born inventors. Our cumulative efforts have brought us from the stone age to the wonders of today's civilization. The

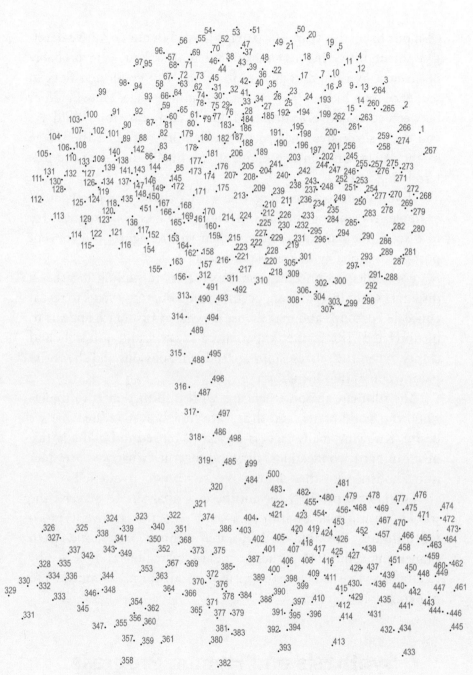

FIGURE 5.1 Connect the Dots to See What Emerges

inventions and advances that have shaped that extraordinary journey have not come out of thin air. Every single one has built on ideas, research, and insight that came before.

All innovation stems from connecting existing ideas in new ways.

The highly eccentric chemist Kary Mullis won the Nobel Prize in 1993 for his breakthrough origination of the polymerase chain reaction (PCR) technique. Speaking about how he came up with the idea, Mullis said, "I put together elements that were already there, but that's what inventors always do. You can't make up new elements, usually. The new element, if any, was the combination, the way they were used."[2] His act of synthesis in inventing PCR is still helping people millions of times every day through its application in the most accurate Covid-19 tests.

In his book *A Whole New Mind*, Daniel Pink argues that we have already moved beyond the information age into the conceptual age, meaning our skills must also evolve. "The future belongs to a very different kind of person with a very different kind of mind—creators and empathizers, pattern recognizers, and meaning makers," he says.[3]

Among the aptitudes Pink puts at the center of success in this era is what he calls "symphonic thinking." "Symphony . . . is the ability to put together the pieces," Pink writes. "It is the capacity to synthesize rather than to analyze; to see relationships between seemingly unrelated fields; to detect broad patterns rather than to deliver specific answers; and to invent something new by combining elements nobody else thought to pair."[4]

As complexity increases, it becomes harder to bring into harmony the cacophony of incessant noise that surrounds us. Synthesis is moving to the center of value creation. It is a capability that we can—and must—actively develop.

Outcomes from Synthesis

Many people "cannot see the forest for the trees," seeing details but never the whole. Global competition and advancing machine capabilities are consistently tearing down the value of those people who see only minutiae, and steadily increasing the value of those who grasp higher-level systems. Those who are adept at synthesis will be masters of the universe. There are five primary outcomes from developing your capabilities of synthesis:

1. **Understanding.** Life is a process of sense-making, literally making sense of how the world works, what our place in the world could be, and what things mean. As individuals wending our way through life and work, our primary intent must be to understand the nature of the world and our area of expertise. Everything else flows from there.

2. **True expertise.** Being an expert is of course far more than knowing profuse details about your domain. Pulling together the many elements of your area of expertise, to have seen them from many angles, to see how they all fit together, is at the core of mastery. This is why you cannot be a true expert in any subject without having spent years in the space. Perceiving the whole is a prerequisite for expertise.

3. **Better decisions.** All significant decisions are complex, with multiple factors, many inherently unknowable. Any choice of action made on the basis of individual elements will likely be flawed. Decisions that are based on comprehension of many factors, the broadest possible context, are far more likely to be successful.

4. **Seeing opportunities.** As long as the universe is changing, there will be opportunities. Given today's pace of change, there are more possibilities than ever before. At the same time, perceiving and assessing them becomes far more difficult, given multiplying variables and uncertainties.

Being able to see the whole not only makes opportunities more apparent but also makes evaluating them far more tractable.

5. **Keeping ahead of machines.** AI has transcended expert human capabilities in a host of domains, including recognizing images, diagnosing a range of diseases, and playing virtually every game ever created. Yet humans' ability to synthesize disparate information from disconnected fields to generate understanding, new perspectives, and better decisions far exceeds the capacity of any AI system we can envisage for the foreseeable future.

"We are drowning in information, while starving for wisdom," affirmed biologist E. O. Wilson, who has been described as "Darwin's natural heir."[5] "The world henceforth will be run by synthesizers, people able to put together the right information at the right time, think critically about it, and make important choices wisely." If you want to run the world, be a synthesizer.

The outcome of our synthesis is reflected, ultimately, in our mental models. All our thoughts and actions stem from our conceptions of how the world works.[6]

The Models in Your Mind

Warren Buffett, the "Oracle of Omaha," is the front man of Berkshire Hathaway, whose careful investments have consistently outperformed the market for decades, growing in value over one–thousand-fold over the past 40 years. Yet at the company's annual shareholders meeting, sometimes described as the "Woodstock of Capitalists," attended by 40,000 investors, the event is cohosted by his trusted partner from the very first days of the company, Charlie Munger.

Munger is a careful thinker, considering information from all angles before making investments. Among financial market players he is the apostle of developing sound "mental models" for your life and decisions, with the book compiling his thoughts, *Poor Charlie's Almanack* (available only in hardcover for $120), pored over by investors for insights into how his mind works.

> I think it is undeniably true that the human brain must work in models. The trick is to have your brain work better than the other person's brain because it understands the most fundamental models: ones that will do most work per unit.[7]
>
> **—Charlie Munger**

Cognitive psychologists have long used the idea of mental models—representations in our mind of how the world works—to understand how we think.[8] From the moment we are born, we begin to build models in our minds, starting with how our parents respond to us and the mechanics of the world, before moving on to more complex situations. All our behaviors and every decision we make are based on these models, which tell us what we expect to happen as a result of our actions.

Implicit Wisdom

Many use the term "mental model" to refer to simple frameworks or heuristics that help us to think and make decisions. One example is Occam's razor, which in essence says the solution with fewer elements or assumptions is more likely to be true. It can very handily be applied to many conspiracy theories. Some believers in a flat earth propose that Australia doesn't actually exist—it is a hoax carefully created to deceive us, with those who are supposed to be Australians in fact actors paid by NASA. While this is conceivably true (unless you happen to live in Australia), the myriad activities that would be required to maintain this appearance makes this unlikely, to put it mildly.

Thinking tools such as Occam's razor can certainly be useful, but they do not describe how we actually think. The reality is that we always make decisions based on the entirety of our life's experience and how we have interpreted it. We might use some tools and frameworks to help our conscious decision-making process, but the truth is that our mental models are never fully explicit or understood, even by ourselves.

We will always know more than we can articulate.[9] If we can say it or write it, it becomes information, available to others. But writing or trying to capture in software what we think doesn't make us redundant. We are the sum of our life's experience, able to gain insight and act effectively in situations we have never before encountered. More than looking for simple, reducible rules of thumb to assist our thinking, we should focus holistically on our models as expressing the entirety of our cognition of the world and how we think and act. We will never be able to fully surface or understand our mental models. Yet we can work to improve them, make them more useful, and most importantly, evolve as new information becomes available.

The Wellspring of Synthesis

There are five foundational elements that support our ability to excel at synthesis: openness to ideas, creative connections, integrative thinking, richer mental models, and states of mind for insight. Figure 5.2 depicts how these elements build up from the underlying principles step by step to form an abundant fountainhead of synthesis. Each of these capabilities in turn flows back down to feed the ones below. The synthesis that emerges supports our final outcome: the decisions and actions that are most likely to achieve our goals.

We will delve into each of these elements in turn, beginning from the foundations. The base of the wellspring of synthesis is the simple act of being open to new possibilities and ideas. When today is different from yesterday and tomorrow will be different from today, you cannot rely solely on ideas and experiences of the past and must be receptive to evolving your thinking.

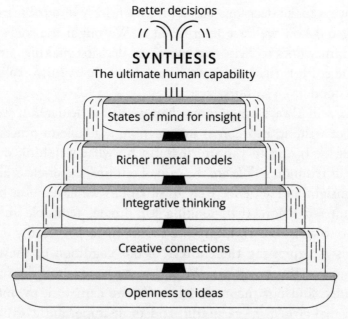

Better decisions

SYNTHESIS
The ultimate human capability

States of mind for insight

Richer mental models

Integrative thinking

Creative connections

Openness to ideas

FIGURE 5.2 The Wellspring of Synthesis

Openness to Ideas

The science of personality types began in 1917 when Katharine Briggs became intrigued by the seemingly unlikely romance between her only daughter Isabel and the young lawyer Clarence Gates Myers. She sought to understand their compatibility and retain her relationship with her daughter. Finally stumbling across Carl Gustav Jung's book *Psychological Types*, she worked with her daughter to create the Myers-Briggs Type Indicator.[10] Over a century later the test is still widely used despite being superseded by superior models.

Researchers have since exhaustively explored and consolidated the full range of human psychological variation into a set of five dimensions, now commonly called the OCEAN "Big Five" personality traits: Openness to experience, Conscientiousness, Extroversion, Agreeableness, and Neuroticism.[11]

Of particular interest to us is openness to experience. This can also be framed as openness to new information: our ability to adapt by noticing that the world has changed, accepting rather than rejecting relevant signals, and as a result, changing our outlook, opinions, and actions. In a swiftly evolving world, people who are less open to new information are significantly disadvantaged, mired in fixed thinking. Those who are open to new ideas and use them to improve their mental models will thrive.

> *In a world of accelerating change the*
> *open-minded have a powerful advantage.*

The empirically demonstrated value of higher openness to experience is massive, including improved job performance, probability of being promoted, and likelihood to become and succeed at being an entrepreneur.[12] Other demonstrated benefits include increased life satisfaction and reduced risk of cognitive decline with age.[13] Not least, it is associated with our ability to perceive salient patterns in a chaotic environment.[14]

Most people think they are open-minded, with 95 percent rating themselves as more open than average.[15] This clearly cannot be true. What distinguishes true leaders and experts is that they work to overcome their inbuilt biases to continually evolve their thinking.

For a long time, psychologists observed that people's personality traits do not usually change substantially over time. However, more recent studies have focused on those who intentionally strive to shape their personality, finding that we can with volition and carefully designed interventions evolve how we engage with the world.[16] If we choose, we can change our personality to make us better adapted to our environment and lead better lives.

There are a variety of proven ways to increase our openness. Exposing ourselves to cultural experiences such as art galleries, museums, and live music performances leads to increased openness to experience, according to a Dutch study of over 7,000 people. This inclination feeds on itself, leading to greater desire for cultural experiences.[17] A range of training courses have been developed that successfully increase openness.[18] However, simply resolving to enact an attitude of being more open for its benefits is often the most effective path.

A recent explosion of research on the impact of psychedelic drugs has uncovered their positive potential in treating a range of maladies, including addiction, anxiety, and depression. Studies on the use of MDMA in the treatment of PTSD and the effects of psilocybin, the active ingredient in "magic mushrooms," showed their therapeutic value was achieved largely through effecting a lasting increase in openness to experience, itself made possible by being receptive to new approaches.[19] Tim Ferriss reports that "the billionaires I know, almost without exception, use hallucinogens on a regular basis," to help them "ask completely new questions."[20] Be aware that this path is not for everyone; there can be significant risks from taking these substances. The studies mentioned were all run by trained therapists in carefully designed environments; this is not a recommendation to take illicit drugs.

The key point to take away is that openness is a foundational driver of success. As the world accelerates this will become even more true. Critically, you can choose to increase it. We should, of course, be aware that there is such a thing as too much openness.

Balancing Openness and Credulity

Have you seen the man in the moon? Magnetic lava flows below the lunar surface have created what for centuries many European cultures have seen as the eyes and mouth of a man. However, next time the moon waxes, look for the rabbit in the moon. East Asian cultures and some indigenous American peoples see a rabbit on our satellite's surface, and once you've seen it, you are likely to see it again every time you gaze at the full moon.

These are simple examples of apophenia, the profoundly human tendency to see patterns where they do not exist. As we discovered in Chapter 2, humans are essentially pattern recognition animals: we perceive patterns so we can respond effectively to the world. The old proverb tells us that "when all you have is a hammer, everything looks like a nail." Our extraordinarily developed pattern-recognition capabilities mean we tend to see patterns in everything, whether they are real or not. This is evident in every aspect of human society, not just in conspiracy theories and quirky cold remedies, but also in our interpersonal interactions and often even business strategies.

The patterns we infer, consciously or often unconsciously, become part of the mental models we use to guide our lives, so we need to be prudent in assessing whether what we believe we see is founded in reality. We must be open to possibilities but also critical in assessing even our own perceptions and ideas. This is perhaps the most central of the many paradoxes we must reconcile to prosper in a deeply complex world. It is up to each of us to negotiate daily Carl Sagan's exhortation to balance an expansive openness to new frames of thinking with intense skepticism.

Being open to new information, albeit judiciously, is the starting point. The next step is forming links between fresh ideas and our existing universe of thinking. We need to go beyond the obvious to identify useful associations, seeing not just the subtle but also the inspired connections.

Creative Connections

When scientists set out to measure creativity, they usually use tests of divergent thinking or remote association. These assess how obvious, unexpected, or diverse the concepts generated from a given starting point are. Some people have let themselves become sadly predictable in their thinking. Others are deeply original and innovative in the connections they bring to life; they are the creators in our society.

> *All synthesis is creative,*
> *and all creativity entails synthesis.*

Perceiving obscure links between disparate ideas is a deeply creative act. The knowledge embodied in the frameworks you built in Chapter 2 came from identifying connections between ideas. The quality of your thinking will be vastly improved if you tend to notice quirkier yet still meaningful associations. Fortunately, you can develop the priceless gift of seeing connections.

Keith Johnstone, widely regarded as the godfather of improvisational theater, often called impro or improv, sees adults as "atrophied children" who have lost the ability to play and communicate directly. He believes that we are all exceptionally creative, it is just that capability has often been stifled in our upbringing and social conditioning.[21]

Improv requires consistent spontaneity, keeping the skit unfolding whither it may go. Participating in improv lessons can do wonders for our ability to transcend our internal censors and make inspired connections. In my twenties I took improvisational theater classes, which definitely helped my personality and ideas to flow more freely. Alternatively, you can find in Johnstone's wonderful book *Impro* many fun and formative games you can play with friends or your children. A simple example is word-at-a-time, in which a group makes up a story, each person in turn swiftly providing the next word in the tale.[22]

Before becoming CEO of Twitter, Dick Costolo studied with Chicago's famed Second City improvisational theater troupe, where actors such as Steve Carell and Tina Fey also trained, later applying what he learned to his corporate leadership style.[23] Renowned Harvard Business School professor Rosabeth Moss Kanter uses improvisational theater as a compelling metaphor to describe how outperforming companies approach strategy.[24]

There are a range of other tools we can use to open our thinking to potential associations. Thinking about or being around people who are unlike you, whether in dress, attitude, or behavior, what researchers describe as "deviancy cues," has been shown to stimulate more creative thinking.[25] The more palpable workplace diversity, the greater the stimulation to innovate.

Psychological distance primes breadth of thought. Spending a moment thinking about places that are far away or what might happen in the distant future engenders big-picture thinking, helping you discern what's important.[26] You can deliberately practice divergent thinking. Many facilitators use decks of cards that present a set of highly diverse concepts. They task participants with generating connections from the issues they are grappling with to the ideas on the cards, sometimes resulting in breakthrough ideas. You can buy these sets of cards or make your own, exercising your ability to make more expansive mental connections.

Reinforcing Variability

The behaviorist B. F. Skinner proposed that all human behavior comes from conditioning, with consistent rewards resulting in predictable behavior. The backlash to this mindset led a generation to shy away from reinforcing human behaviors, feeling it made us akin to Pavlov's dogs that salivated on the ring of a bell.

One of Skinner's graduate students at Harvard, Allen Neuringer, wondered whether reinforcement could encourage variable rather than consistent responses. Through a lifetime of research, he clearly demonstrated that you could train both animals and humans to generate highly unpredictable responses. Earlier studies had shown that dolphins could be encouraged to enact multiple behaviors never before observed in the species, such as an aerial corkscrew.[27] In his relentless self-experimentation, Neuringer used conditioning feedback to mentally generate random numbers, something previously thought impossible. A wide range of other experiments have verified that we can reinforce in ourselves creative, divergent responses.[28] We can positively shape our thinking patterns.

You can choose to make divergent, unpredictable thinking a habit.

The highest level of creative association is linking ideas that seem to be not only unconnected, but in fact contradictory. As novelist F. Scott Fitzgerald observed, "the test of a first-rate intelligence is the ability to hold two opposed ideas in mind at the same time and still retain the ability to function."[29] In an exceptionally complex world we need commensurately sophisticated mental models. This means they are increasingly likely to encompass what appear to be paradoxes.

Integrative Thinking

Sporting two faces looking in opposite directions, Janus was the Roman god of beginnings and endings, doorways, transitions, and polarities. The first of January, the month bearing his name, is both an ending and a beginning, representing opposites combined into a unity. The capacity for integrative thinking at the heart of synthesis is at its most creative and powerful when uniting paradoxes and polarities.

> *Life at its best is a creative synthesis of opposites in fruitful harmony.*
> —**Martin Luther King Jr.**

Paradoxical thinking is a skill you can develop that turns out to have manifold benefits. The Red Queen instructed Alice that with practice you can believe in impossible things. "When I was your age,

I always did it for half-an-hour a day," she said. "Why, sometimes I've believed as many as six impossible things before breakfast."[30]

A study by Ella Miron-Spektor, now a professor at leading business school INSEAD, tested the outcomes of this practice, confirming "the positive influence of paradoxical frames on creativity," reporting that those primed to think of paradoxes, "increase exploration, sensitivity to unusual associations, and generation of new associations."[31] A follow-up study by Miron-Spektor showed that employees in a large American company who had a "paradox mindset" were seen by their managers to be more innovative and perform better in their roles.[32]

Many of the most valuable innovations in business stem from pursuing paradoxical objectives, such as simultaneously making things more profitable and better for the environment, or cheaper and higher quality. When Mother Teresa had a heart attack in 1984, specialist Dr. Devi Shetty took care of her, becoming her physician for the last five years of her life. She inspired him to turn his skills to helping the poor.[33] He set out to provide the highest-quality medical attention at the lowest possible cost, serving anyone who needs care irrespective of their ability to pay. He founded what became Narayana Health in 2000 with a 300-bed hospital in Kolkata. The organization has now grown to 46 healthcare institutions with over 6,000 beds, generating a market capitalization of well over $1 billion. Its heart surgery procedures have by some measures better health outcomes than US hospitals, with heart bypasses delivered at 2 percent of the cost.[34]

A study of 22 Nobel Prize winners showed they all demonstrated "Janus thinking," which the paper's author defined as "actively conceiving multiple opposites or antitheses simultaneously." Obvious examples include Niels Bohr's epiphany that quantum objects can manifest either as waves or particles and Einstein's reconciliation of Newtonian gravity with relativity, which he described as "the happiest thought of my life."[35] Discontinuous scientific progress is almost always through bold synthesis of domains that have been previously considered distinct.

The very phrase "thriving on overload" represents a paradox. Through this book we have examined some of the many paradoxes we must successfully integrate on this path, including openness and discernment, detail and big picture, clarity and seeking, and many more. As you work to develop your capabilities for success in our chaotic world, be sure to apply a paradox mindset.

In improvisational theater, a central principle is that you never negate what you are offered; you always take it and build on it, wherever that might take you. It is never "no" or "but," it is unfailingly "yes, and." This attitude is intrinsic to creative integration, recognizing that even opposites can be reconciled. We can inculcate in ourselves an attitude of integrating all worthy ideas, whether they appear to confirm or contradict what we already know. We only sometimes want to replace old ideas with new ones; more often we want to add complementary perspectives. The ability to bring together diverse viewpoints into a richer, more sophisticated whole is at the center of continually improving your mental models in an increasingly complex world.

Richer Mental Models

"All models are wrong," noted seminal statistician George Box, "but it is only necessary that they be useful."[36] Some mental models are certainly useful, as has been proven amply true for Charlie Munger. Some people's models of the world are definitely dysfunctional, as you no doubt will have observed through the course of your life.

What makes our mental models useful or otherwise depends on the context. If you have a simple decision to make, such as whether to take an umbrella with you when you go out, basic mental models are likely to be more useful than elaborate ones. On the other hand, if you are dealing with complex issues such as making strategic decisions in rapidly evolving industries, embarking on a career in the 2020s, or shaping government policies, you will need sophisticated thinking to achieve good outcomes.

Our mental models are necessarily imperfect, and the world is constantly changing. They must evolve; we need to make them richer by including more—and more diverse—elements. The severe challenge we face is to continuously refine our mental models, while retaining the value of the lessons we have learned through a lifetime of experience.

Evolving Our Thinking

Famed economist John Maynard Keynes was highly inclined, almost eager, to alter his opinions, reputedly responding to a critic of his fickleness, "When my information changes, I change my mind. What do you do?"[37] Economics is certainly a field in which information from the past is incomplete, new data is constantly flowing in, and carefully constructed models will not necessarily hold in what will inevitably be a different future. Yet even in the "hard" sciences such as physics, experts uncover new information and need to evolve or sometimes completely change their views.

Science historian Thomas Kuhn's book *The Structure of Scientific Revolutions*, frequently cited as one of the best nonfiction books of all time, describes the nature of how an established orthodoxy goes through a number of phases until a new paradigm becomes current.[38] As contrary evidence to the existing view becomes available, defenders and challengers of the traditional framework tussle, going through a stage of crisis until a new widely accepted paradigm emerges.

Obvious examples include the Copernican Revolution, gradually progressing to understanding that the Earth is not the center of the universe, and various Einsteinian conceptual shifts, including the transition from Newtonian physics to general relativity.

We need to apply exactly the same process to our personal models and frames we use to understand the world. We need to acknowledge opposing information, strive to reconcile it with our existing frameworks, and if necessary, evolve our models or sometimes completely throw out old ones to adopt a more useful way of thinking about the world.

Being Right by Being Wrong

"The smartest people are constantly revising their understanding, reconsidering a problem they thought they'd already solved," according to Amazon founder Jeff Bezos. "They're open to new points of view, new information, new ideas, contradictions, and challenges to their own way of thinking."[39] He has a low opinion of those who are too set in their thinking. "Anyone who doesn't change their mind a lot is dramatically underestimating the complexity of the world," he says.[40]

What researchers call "actively open-minded thinking" requires not just being open to new information, but deliberately seeking input that could challenge existing ways of thinking. This extremely rewarding capability requires disconnecting your knowledge and beliefs from your identity.

Separate your knowledge from your personal identity to become a better thinker.

If you think of yourself as a highly knowledgeable expert, you may see challenges to your views as personal attacks. As meta-entrepreneur Paul Graham notes, "people can never have a fruitful argument about something that's part of their identity."[41]

If, in contrast, your identity is that you are always eager to learn and update your understanding, you will consider contradictory information as an opportunity to improve your mental models. Respected technology analyst Ben Thompson says, "I am wrong all the time, and I relish the opportunity to say when I'm wrong." As he observes industry developments, he checks them against his highly developed mental models. He usually finds they fit, but it is most interesting to him when they don't. He practices his "discipline to avoid confirmation biases" so he doesn't discount evidence his thinking is incorrect, and can thus consistently expand his worldview. "If you want to be right, admit you're wrong," he says.[42]

Rounding out the five key principles that underlie synthesis is nurturing enabling states of mind. We can learn to evoke the conditions for insight.

States of Mind for Insight

Philo Farnsworth grew up in Idaho. As a youth his parents and teachers could already see he had the makings of genius, but he still had to help out by plowing the potato fields. In 1920, at age 14, as he toiled and surveyed the furrows filled with lines of potatoes, it occurred to him that images could be transmitted at a distance by communicating lines of information, with each potato representing a degree of brightness, and a scan of each line in turn resulting in recreating a live image at a distance. He immediately set to work to bring his epiphany to reality. Eight years later he had built the first functional television.[43]

There are legion tales of powerful insight achieved, not when striving, but when in more relaxed frames of mind. Archimedes was reputedly in the bath when he solved the problem of assessing whether the gold in the king's crown had been adulterated, August Kekulé was daydreaming when he intuited the circular molecular structure of benzene, while Nietzsche proclaimed, "It is only ideas gained from walking that have any worth."

Insight is hard to study, as it so often turns up unannounced. When John Kounios and Mark Beeman first met, they connected through their shared fascination of the potential for neuroimaging to study the evanescent experience of insight. Given their limited resources, they could run only one experiment to prove their intuition. As the results came in, they were delighted to find their instincts proven correct; they had for the first time demonstrated the neurological foundation of the "aha" moment.[44]

They discovered that specific patterns of brain waves are associated with insight. It is almost a century since we learned that there are distinct sets of frequencies for human neuronal activity, ranging from the delta range of 1–4 cycles per second present during some phases of sleep through to the high gamma range of up to 150 Hertz. Each of the frequencies correlate to different states of mind, with, for example, theta waves (4–8 Hertz) associated with memory formation and deep meditation, alpha waves (8–12 Hertz) present while we are relaxed and calm, and high-band beta (18–20 Hertz) observed during intense active thinking.

Kounios and Beeman found that the moment of insight is associated with a short burst of gamma waves. At the same time, blood flows to the anterior cingulate, located under the prefrontal cortex behind our forehead, which is linked to making distant connections such as understanding humor and metaphors.[45] When this part of the brain is active you are more likely to generate creative connections.

What they were surprised to learn is that the flash of insight is directly preceded by a brief alpha state. As they came to understand its function, they called it a "brain blink" during which the brain goes into idle, attenuating visual input to reduce distraction.[46] To help gestating thoughts emerge, people often turn inside, closing their eyes or defocusing. Our brains sometimes also spontaneously act to create the mental conditions for inspired connections.

Creating the Conditions for Insight

Getting into the right frame of mind is necessary for powerful synthesis. Your most valuable insights are likely to happen when your brain is in alpha or theta state, which in our busy world is becoming less common and needs to be nurtured. We can act to cultivate our ability to synthesize.

Nolan Bushnell, founder of gaming trailblazer Atari, noted, "Everyone who's ever taken a shower has an idea." He goes on to specify that "it's the person who gets out of the shower, dries off, and does something about it who makes a difference." Indeed, every successful venture requires novel thinking followed by concerted action.

Showers and baths are widely perceived to be where ideas spring to mind. This happens to be where we are usually in a state of relaxation, with often mid-alpha brain waves, in the pleasure of the moment of the warm water, our thoughts straying whither they will. Some companies sell waterproof notepads and pencils so we can take notes in one of the places where compelling ideas are most likely to arise.

Kounios and Beeman explain why showers are so conducive to insight. "The white noise of the running water is hard to focus on and blocks out other kinds of sounds. The warm water makes it difficult for you to feel the boundary between the interior and exterior of your body, so your sense of touch recedes from awareness. The visual inputs are unchanging and blurry. Perhaps your eyes are even closed to keep the soap out. Taking a shower is an excellent way to cut off the environment, focus your thoughts inwardly, and have an insight."[47]

Walks in nature facilitate the "soft fascination" described by the Kaplans in Chapter 4, not only allowing us to regenerate our ability to focus, but also putting us in an appropriate state of mind for synthesis. Many people who exercise more vigorously by running, swimming, or cycling for extended periods often experience a state of mind similar to meditators. Marathon runners in the midst of their 26-mile odyssey tend to greater front theta and global alpha brain waves, which are also strongly associated with insight.[48]

The brilliant and idiosyncratic Ludwig Wittgenstein, whose book *Philosophical Investigations* has been cited as the most important philosophy book of the twentieth century, reportedly said that creative thinking depends on the three Bs: bed, bath, and bus.[49] At their best, buses and trains have similar characteristics to showers or baths: lulling sounds, defocused attention, and comfort. Being snug in bed offers a similar opportunity for your mind to wander and happen upon unexpected connections.

Hypnagogia is the hinterland between wakefulness and sleep, when fragments of the dreaming state start to enter your consciousness. Many people in this state startle back awake when an idea comes to mind, sometimes to make a note before the thought is lost. Surrealist painter Salvador Dalí, not surprisingly given his dreamlike art, was heavily inspired by the "repose which walks in equilibrium on the taut and invisible wire which separates sleeping from waking." Technology futurist Cathy Hackl reports that insights often come unbidden when she is going to sleep. "All of a sudden, boom, it's there and connection is made; I totally understand, and I see something I didn't see before," she reports.[50]

Inventor Thomas Edison worked late and long, but also napped most days, waiting for the next brilliant idea to strike him. In a technique also used by Dalí, he rested and held a steel ball in his hand poised above a metal plate. When the ball fell out of his hand he woke and immediately wrote down the ideas that had come to mind.[51] President John F. Kennedy combined some of these techniques, often having an afternoon nap as well as two hot baths each day.

Seeding and Incubating

When a chick pecks its way out of its shell, it does not appear out of nowhere. It has sat for an extended period in conducive conditions, nurtured to the point where it is ready to come forth into the world. Creative synthesis often comes to us in a moment, however, usually after extended gestation in our unconscious minds. When we struggle with a conceptual problem for a long time, it is commonplace for the answer to spring to mind when we are doing something completely different. Our brain has been working for us while we pay attention to other things, engaging in "opportunistic assimilation" of perspectives and ideas relevant to the problem it is trying to solve.[52]

Knowing that synthesis requires incubation allows us to carefully plant the seeds of ideas and tend to them so they are most likely to bear beautiful fruit. When we are struggling with a problem, if we cannot solve it on the spot we should aim to surface as many outlooks on the challenge as possible, providing our unconscious mind with better raw materials for incubation, then do something else.

Nikola Tesla was one of the many inventors who implicitly understood this. "I may go on for months or years with the idea in the back of my head," he said. "Whenever I feel like it, I roam around in my imagination and think about the problem without any deliberate concentration. This is a period of incubation."[53]

In turn, plant seeds through focused thinking and cultivate them through expansive states of mind.

These two states feed on each other; they only have true value in conjunction. A facility for evoking and switching between different frames of mind is a powerful enabler of synthesis. Kounios and Beeman propose that "alternating between the inner and outer worlds is the best way to enhance your creativity."[54]

The ultimate value of our ability to synthesize information and refine our mental models is in our actions. We need to apply the full ambit of the insight we have developed to making better decisions.

Informed Decisions in an Uncertain World

John Boyd signed up for the Army Air Corps at age 17 in the final year of World War II, training as a pilot and flying in Korea as an F-86 pilot. After his tour of duty, he was inducted into the Fighter Weapon School, took top marks, and was asked to become an instructor at the academy.

His self-confidence was legendary. He threw out a standing bet that he could trounce any comer in simulated air-to-air combat within 40 seconds, offering $40 to anyone who could beat him. Many took up the challenge, but Boyd never had to take out his wallet.[55] His superlative ability was based not on his reflexes, but on the quality of his mental models.

Throughout his life Boyd sought to build frameworks for high-pressure decision-making that could be taught and studied. Among these he proposed the OODA loop, connecting the four phases of Observe, Orient, Decide, and Act into a virtuous cycle of learning. The idea was developed to help fighter pilots defeat their opponents, but decades later the OODA loop is also applied extensively in business and engineering. Notably it was a central inspiration for the Lean Startup loop that sits at the center of the strategy of virtually every startup in Silicon Valley and beyond.[56] Boyd had highlighted that making effective decisions involves continual learning as well as action.

Decision-making requires synthesizing the information you have, but always entails uncertainty. For example, if you are considering investing in an early-stage startup, you will undoubtedly be shown a snappily designed presentation including jaw-dropping revenue forecasts. If you ask the right questions, hopefully the founders will be able to provide the specific assumptions on which their targets are based. Whatever you are told, the degree of uncertainty in the company's prospects is huge, and you will never have enough information to be confident in the fate of your investment. But if you use that as a reason to walk away or wait until there is more evidence, you may be missing out on a runaway success. How should you make a decision? Let us examine some frames on decision-making that may be helpful.

Iterative Decisions

Herbert Simon coined the neologism "satisfice" to describe decisions that sufficed to satisfy a threshold of acceptability. Historically, economists and psychologists have liked to assume humans are utterly rational and have perfect information. Fortunately, most now acknowledge that humans are rarely fully logical, and we seldom have all the information we want.

In fact, more information is not necessarily better. Former secretary of state Colin Powell declared, "I can make a decision with 30 percent of the information. Anything more than 80 percent is too much."

Gathering and assessing information has a real cost, not least in time and cognitive processing. An essential choice for all decision makers is whether they should make a decision with the information they already have available, or they need more input. In an uncertain environment the best way to proceed—if at all possible—is to make smaller decisions that will yield information to improve subsequent and potentially larger decisions. The faster the pace of change, the greater the potential cost of delaying decisions and the higher the premium on swift action.

> *Formulate decisions that will make you
> better informed for your next decision.*

This is at the core of the lesson John Boyd derived from his experience training the world's best fighter pilots. His OODA loop, depicted in Figure 5.3, describes the process of learning from your decisions and actions. To improve performance, decisions must result in outcomes you can observe and learn from, designed to surface whatever information will be most valuable for your next decision. As much as possible make iterative decisions, building on lessons learned from previous ones.

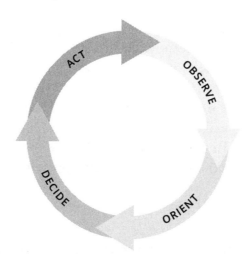

FIGURE 5.3 OODA Loop for Iterative Decision-Making

Decisions as Bets

As you learned in Chapter 3, the Bayesian approach of thinking in probabilities is immensely valuable in filtering information. It allows us to move past considering new information as either confirming or invalidating our beliefs. We can instead assess how it might adjust our mental models and assessments.

This mindset is just as relevant in decision-making. By definition all decisions deal with uncertainty. The only appropriate response is to think explicitly in terms of probabilities.

Shortly before completing her PhD dissertation in cognitive psychology, Annie Duke fell ill, took a leave of absence, married, and moved to rural Montana. Her funds were running out, so she learned to play poker to pay the bills, starting out in the basement of a local bar. She never returned to her formal studies, but thought of poker as a "new kind of lab for studying how people learn and make decisions." In her subsequent career as a professional poker player she ended up winning over $4 million and a range of major tournaments, including the World Series of Poker Tournament of Champions, going on to advise senior executives on how to improve their decision-making.[57]

Poker provides a strong analogy for many real-world decisions. Holding your cards and deciding your play, you face significant risk, partial information, and other participants with unpredictable and sometimes deceptive behaviors. Whenever you place a bet, take a card, or fold, it should be based on your assessment of the odds.

"Getting comfortable with 'I'm not sure' is a vital step to being a better decision maker," says Duke. "We have to make peace with not knowing."[58] This is hard, but in an increasingly unpredictable world, we must acknowledge the reality of uncertainty.

More than ever, leaders and decision makers need to not just accept but embrace ambiguity.

The 2020s have taught us, if we didn't already know, that striving to make the world knowable is a fool's errand. Conceding uncertainty frees us to make assessments based on limited information, examining all perspectives on our possible actions. Starting with a careful evaluation of probabilities lets us place our stakes more wisely.

"Thinking in bets triggers a more open-minded exploration of alternative hypotheses, of reasons supporting conclusions opposite to the routine of self-serving bias," believes Duke. "We are more likely to explore the opposite side of an argument more often and more seriously—and that will move us closer to the truth of the matter."[59]

Consider the Opposite

Professor Rick Larrick of Duke University specializes in the subtle and challenging art of "debiasing," helping people move beyond their biases. He draws on decades of extensive research that confirms the most promising approach is the simple yet powerful approach of "consider the opposite," asking yourself, "What are some reasons that my initial judgment might be wrong?"[60]

This apparently modest exercise has been shown to reduce a variety of biases, including overconfidence. The value of this is underlined by Daniel Kahneman's statement that overconfidence is the "most damaging" of the multitude of biases that afflict us.

In the nineteenth century the Prussian army brought together a divided Germany, in the process defeating France, Austria, and Denmark. The Prussians' success was attributed in part to their innovative use of war gaming to temper their strategies. On their boards the Prussian army was represented by blue blocks to indicate the famous Prussian blue uniforms worn by their soldiers. The teams playing the enemy used red blocks to indicate their regiments, giving rise to the phase "red teams" to describe groups who are tasked with finding flaws and problems with strategies. The longstanding use of red team exercises by the US military has increased significantly since the September 11 attacks.[61]

Similar approaches are now common in large investment management firms. The cost of making a bad decision can be enormous, so you need to test decisions against the unexpected. "It's the responsibility of everybody else in the room to stress test the thinking," says Marc Andreessen of the decision-making process of leading venture capital firm Andreessen Horowitz. "If necessary, we'll create a red team. We'll formally create the countervailing force and designate some set of people to counterargue the other side."[62]

Hedge fund Bridgewater, led by Ray Dalio, is one of the most successful investors in the world, managing $160 billion and over 28 years averaging double the returns of the S&P 500. Forceful questioning by employees of suggested investments or others' opinions is not just tolerated, it is expected, to ensure decisions are fully robust. Adam Grant, who has studied the firm's processes, says of Bridgewater, "You get rated on whether you are challenging your boss. . . . They basically evaluate you on whether you're fighting for right, even when other people disagree."[63] At Netflix everyone is expected to actively seek different opinions before major decisions; CEO Reed Hastings calls this "farming for dissent."[64]

Let's look at how you could apply these lessons to whether to invest in the early-stage startup introduced earlier. First, you should acknowledge your investment is a bet that you may win or lose, and your task is simply to use all information available to assess the likelihood of success. You might ask someone who knows the industry to help identify the reasons the startup might fail. The greatest value from that will be seeing if the founders have already considered these issues, demonstrating the openness of their thinking, and have decent responses. Or you might make a smaller initial investment so that you can access company reporting and have better information to decide whether to invest more in subsequent rounds.

In an increasingly complex and uncertain world, the vital skills of synthesis are fundamental not just to your life, career, and ventures, but far beyond. We need to get better at synthesis, individually and collectively, to create a better future.

Synthesis and the Future of Humanity

In my role as futurist, I often say that as soon as you look far enough into the future of any domain, be it work, retail, homes, healthcare, media, cities, the environment, or anything else, you are essentially considering the future of humanity. Everything in our world is richly intertwined; any subject you can consider is inherently related to everything else.

Synthesis is a profoundly creative act. By bringing together diverse elements in a fresh way, you forge a new reality. And in that generative act you cannot help but bring to bear the full scope of who you are and your perception of the world.

Synthesis is precisely about perceiving the entirety, comprehensively taking into account everything that is relevant. This includes the role of people and the broader context of our planet in which we are set. One reason humans will always transcend machines in their ability to synthesize is that they can empathize and comprehend the implications for humans in ways algorithms never can. Seeing the whole is essential to understand what is possible and the paths that lead there.

The capacity for synthesis sits at the heart of our ability to create a better future for ourselves and humanity.

More of us improving our capabilities at synthesis will maximize the chances that our collective future will be better rather than worse. As you further develop your power of synthesis, you will inevitably be contributing to a better future for us all.

Integrating the Power of Synthesis

Synthesis is the master key that unlocks the potential of the four other powers, bringing them together to create understanding, insight, and the ability to act effectively in an incredibly complex world. More than ever, it will be the central capability in a rapidly accelerating future of work.

Each of the tiers in the wellspring of synthesis represents skills that we can develop. The future belongs to those open to continually improving their minds and thinking. You can make the choice to change yourself to become better adapted to the state of the twenty-first century. The accompanying benefits include better mental health, happiness, and longevity.

By enhancing your capacity for synthesis, you are now better able to integrate the five powers into a whole that suits you perfectly. This will amplify your ability to prosper in our extraordinary rapidly unfolding world, truly thriving on overload.

EXERCISES

Contrarian Thinking

Identify an issue related to your work where you have a strong opinion but you know some people disagree. Clearly articulate your opinion, then research and develop a strong argument for the contrary case. To make it more challenging, do it for a specific social or political issue.

Active Open-Minded Thinking

What will you do to enhance your capability and propensity for openness to new ideas and different thinking? What thinking habits can you adopt that will help? Are there any activities that might positively shift your openness to experience?

Insight Mode

What activities or behaviors help you get into insight mode? How can you plan these into your day?

Incubating Ideas

Choose a significant decision or conceptual challenge and aim to ready it for incubation. Consider it from as many angles as possible without necessarily looking for a solution. Later, come back to it, and find ways to bring yourself to insight mode. Make this a consistent practice and discover what approaches work best for you.

CHAPTER 6

FROM OVERLOAD TO ABUNDANCE

Integrating the Five Powers

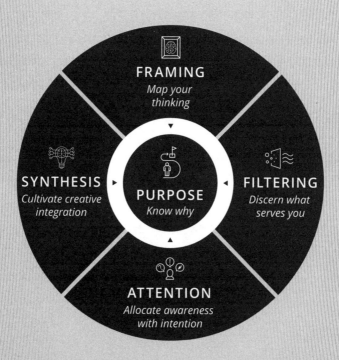

We are called to be architects of the future, not its victims.[1]

—R. Buckminster Fuller, designer, inventor, and author
of *Operating Manual for Spaceship Earth*

The five powers you have learned will best help you thrive, not applied individually, but integrated into a whole that suits your unique mind, thinking, and objectives.

Looking to an information-saturated future of humanity, there are grave risks, not least in intensifying social polarization, but also compelling opportunities, especially in transcending this divide through intelligent education in information skills.

Our brains' neuroplasticity in an information-intensive environment necessarily results in cognitive evolution. The default impact could be negative, but we can choose to develop our cognitive capabilities to become highly adapted to the world in which we live.

We have not chosen to be born into these times of over-abundance, yet we have the choice and now the tools to thrive in this world.

Congratulations on getting this far in the book. You are undoubtedly better equipped, not just to deal effectively with the world of massive overload that we live in, but to thrive on it.

By the accident of when you and I were born we can consider ourselves to be either blessed (my belief) or cursed to live in a world of boundless information. If we were not connected to the world's information, then we couldn't learn from and build on the extraordinary progress, ideas, and insights of innovators everywhere. As it is, every one of us can access a scope of resources absolutely unimaginable a scant few years ago.

This is a remarkable opportunity. Yet the privilege of this superabundance has marked downsides. It comes inextricably tied to the need to sift through the prodigious plenty to find what is relevant, useful, and adds value to our lives. The degree to which information overload is an opportunity or problem is largely up to you and how you approach it.

Whether you prosper or are overwhelmed in our world of excess is, more than anything, a choice.

Choosing to prosper is, in truth, not an easy path. You need to develop and apply the skills and practices outlined in this book, making them part of your daily activities. Where this challenge comes into perspective is in comparison with what might seem like the easy way, the path of least resistance, of letting today's flood of information simply wash over you, taking in whatever snags your attention in the endless stream, a victim to information predators.

In the 2020s and beyond, if you have any ambition or purpose, your success will undoubtedly stem from a superior ability to generate value, insight, and better decisions from unlimited information. Today those achieving exceptional results are—consciously or unconsciously—consistently developing these foundational life skills.

Integrating the Powers

The five powers described in this book are not separate and distinct; they are different facets of a whole: your ability to thrive on overload. This is of course not just about goal achievement or success. It is, ultimately, at least as much about reaching balance, health, and happiness in a frantic world. Overload does not necessarily lead to a feeling of being overwhelmed, but if it does, by its very nature it destroys well-being and the ability to function effectively. Taken together, developing the five powers can move you beyond today's severe challenges to give you a strong feeling of control of your life.

Understanding your *purpose* for engaging with information has to sit at the center of your abilities, relating to and informing how you develop and apply the other powers. *Framing* sets the foundations for synthesis and provides the reference point for your filtering. *Filtering* the signal from the noise is necessarily a central activity and is one of the frames for attention. Being conscious in how we allocate our *attention* is at the heart of self-determination in a world designed to distract you. *Synthesis* pulls together all the other elements to generate what has true value: understanding, insight, and better decisions.

Each power has immense value, but it is in the whole of how they come together that the true potential lies: making your capabilities a match to the extraordinary world in which we live. You need to integrate the powers and their underlying actions and attitudes into who you are and how you behave.

Steps Toward Thriving

Reading this book alone will not lead to excellence. You need to put the ideas into practice, to change what you do day by day based on what you have learned.

The exercises at the end of each chapter are designed to help you establish your own personal plan and odyssey for thriving on overload. If you didn't do them as you read the book, I strongly encourage you to go back to complete the exercises, or at least the ones you think will be most useful. You might wish to write the responses in your own notebooks or online documents rather than in this book so they are easy to refer to without carrying the book around, and allowing you to lend the book to a friend as well!

Downloadable copies of the exercises and an in-depth online course are available at the book website, thrivingonoverload.com. Also look through the Resources for Thriving following this chapter. I point to a range of wonderful books that go deeper into some of the important ideas introduced in this book.

Opportunities for the Future of Overload

The entire history of humanity built up to the recent inflection point of complete information immersion. Where will we go from here? I offer a very safe prediction:

Information overload will inexorably increase through this decade and beyond.

Excessive information is already a defining aspect of our lives and times, but this is just the beginning. Part of the cause lies simply in the continuing acceleration of connectivity and data creation. The more important reason is that humans by their very nature have an insatiable appetite for information. We will never transcend that; we will always want more. The economy has already transitioned from the tangible to the intangible. That shift will inevitably continue as value and work migrate to information-based industries.

This leads to deep challenges as well as opportunities. More information alone is not the biggest problem we face. There are incredibly high incentives to design information that influences us to support others' agendas, not our own best interests. Moreover, AI's growing capacity to manipulate, fed by an avalanche of personal data including how we touch screens, voice stress patterns, and facial emotional cues, is deeply alarming.

These issues lie at the center of our lives and of society at large. We need to carefully consider the implications, and how we can make the best of this state of affairs.

Better Tools

In mid-1998 the most used web search engines included the likes of Yahoo, AltaVista, LookSmart, and Excite. They showed results that were primarily based on the frequency of search terms on the web page, so it was very easy for internet entrepreneurs to engage in "keyword stuffing" to rank well, and hard for users to find the most relevant results for their queries.

Then Google launched in September 1998, with "Beta" boldly stamped on the website to indicate it was not yet a finished product. The founders, Sergey Brin and Larry Page, had invented a metric to indicate the likelihood a given web page would be relevant and useful to the searcher. Within five years it became the most used search engine in the United States.[2]

Problems are the spark for invention. It is safe to say that we have a deep problem in our ability to find the most relevant information and avoid irrelevant or misleading content. We need better tools than we have today.

Part of the reason has been in the creative destruction that has been emblematic of the internet economy, leading to the untimely death of useful platforms such as Delicious and FriendFeed. The rapidly mutating economics of the news industry has also played a role, with a proliferation of aspirant news aggregators, each jostling for a share of advertising revenue, perverting many efforts. The potential value of personalized newsfeeds has been undermined by (usually merited) distrust of the companies that apply behavioral data to peddling advertisements rather than creating value for their users.

There remains a massive opportunity to provide better services to help us filter and find what is most useful to us. It is highly encouraging to see the increasing pool of talent, inspiration, and capital being dedicated to help us discover the most useful information and distinguish between information that is correct, questionable, or plain wrong. I hold strong hopes that in the current mix of contenders in this space some truly valuable services will emerge and prosper.

The Risks of Polarization

In my work as a futurist I must, unfortunately, consistently point to the deep forces driving polarization across societies on a multitude of dimensions, including most evidently income, politics, healthcare, values, wealth, power, openness, and privacy. While the "digital divide" that leaves behind those with inadequate access to information remains critical, the primary danger has shifted to the divergence in our behaviors.

The central thesis of this book is that we have a choice on whether we thrive or are overwhelmed in a world of information excess. As some people take the option of thriving while others follow the path of least resistance, this will aggravate polarization across society, as some become finely adapted to the drivers of success in our emerging world, and others become cannon fodder for the information wars.

"Information abundance, like all markets of abundance, is bad for the average person but great for a small number of people," observes writer David Perell. "The best metaphor is health, where obesity rates and the number of people in incredible shape are *both* rising," he notes.[3]

Improved tools and reduced predatory behavior by information purveyors, be it through social pressure or regulation, will certainly help. However, the most important issue is empowering as many people as possible with the skills that give them choices. We need better information education.

Information Skills on the Curriculum

Throughout the 25 years that I have focused on developing individual information skills, I have been amazed at the incredible paucity of explicit information skills programs, be they at schools or universities, or even in companies where the productivity and effectiveness of their staff depends more than anything on their ability to deal well with information. There are a few programs here and there, but these are almost oddities rather than at the core of skill development, as they should be in the world in which we live.

The first step is simply acknowledging that information capabilities are fundamental to everything we do, our ability to succeed in almost every aspect of our work and many facets of our lives. Stemming from that recognition, educators and leaders must prioritize and architect the programs and working environments that will enhance those skills. The fact is that the most successful people are those who have taught themselves to be effective at making the most of information excess. Yet usually even they, not to mention others, can benefit from explicitly focusing on enhancing their information habits and routines.

Cognitive Evolution

In just longer than a blink of an eye the internet and smartphone have moved to the center of our everyday lives. This has led numerous thinkers and authors, notably Nicholas Carr, Susan Greenfield, and Jason Lanier, to stridently criticize our contemporary use of technology.

"The human brain adapts to the environment and the environment is changing in an unprecedented way, so the brain may also be changing in an unprecedented way," says Greenfield.[4] To my mind this is a truism. It is starkly evident that our highly flexible and neuroplastic minds are incredibly responsive to their environment. There is no question that our brains are evolving in a fast-changing world. Those of adults are changing in response to different stimuli, and children's brains today are developing in different ways than those who were young just a decade or two earlier.

There are, of course, real dangers from this. Greenfield's polemic *Mind Change: How Digital Technologies Are Leaving Their Mark on Our Brains* likens the impact of digital technologies on the brain to climate change.[5] As critics of the book have pointed out, the evidence supporting many of her claims is sparse or contradictory,[6] but she is right to point to the possibility of negative effects and the need for greater research on these. The potential (though not confirmed) impacts she references include reduced attention spans, interpersonal skills, and ability to build deep knowledge.

Yet there is no change that is all good or all bad. On the face of it, if our minds are evolving in response to their changing environment, they are likely to be better suited to it. Minds that were best adapted to the world of the 1970s, for example, would likely not perform as well today. Yet some who were embarking on their working careers then are doing exceptionally well today, having adeptly adjusted to the very different environment they live in today.

As with all technology-driven change, we need to be keenly aware of the possible downsides and finely attuned to the positive potential. There are two major opportunities from living in unprecedented information immersion.

The first opportunity is the ability to judiciously implement "cognitive offloading" by transferring mental tasks to technology.

To take an obvious example, we long ago started using calculators for everyday arithmetic. At the time many claimed we would lose our ability to perform simple math. A more pertinent question is why we should spend our time doing math when our brains are capable of so much more interesting tasks. The concern would be justified if degraded mental math skills impacted other cognitive faculties. In fact, a meta-analysis of 42 studies on the use of calculators in middle and high school through college mathematics courses has found that use of calculators improves conceptual capabilities and mathematical achievement.[7] We can now offload to technology far more complex cognitive tasks, from recognizing cancerous cells in x-ray images to deciding whether an email is likely to be important to us.

We are on the threshold of a new phase in which decisions are offloaded to machines, raising a welter of practical and ethical issues. There are some decisions that we can, with sufficient oversight, simply delegate to AI. However, for many important decisions we will need to bring together the best of natural and artificial intelligence into systems that can outperform each applied alone. Those who become better "cyborgs" by intelligently complementing their higher-order abilities with the rapidly advancing capabilities of machines will forge ahead.

Considering cognitive offloading purely from an information-processing perspective, we can and should expect technologies (sometimes with humans in the loop) to become far better than they are today at services such as identifying content that interests you, assessing the veracity of facts and articles, or even providing pointed counterarguments to your investment theses.

> *The second and bigger opportunity*
> *is to consciously and positively guide*
> *your personal cognitive evolution.*

Your brain will inevitably evolve. In 10 years from now it will be significantly different. It will have changed in response to the likely expansion of your information immersion, and more importantly, how you choose to respond to that environment, including your daily information habits. Adopting effective behaviors will lead your brain to develop to better suit a world of abundance. If you enact the suggestions offered in this book, especially those in Chapter 4 on attention, you will be assisting your neurology to adapt successfully.

The relatively new science of epigenetics has uncovered that our genes are expressed differently depending on our environment and behavior.[8] In other words, how you respond to information excess will change who you are. If your behaviors suit your evolving environment, you will become better adapted. Studies of transgenerational epigenetics show that these changes can be passed down to your offspring.[9] Your personal evolution can directly benefit your children.

Thriving Today and Tomorrow

Information excess is a defining attribute of our times. Personally, I am overjoyed to have virtually unlimited information access, compared to the alternative of information being restricted or difficult to access. This is an incredible boon to us all. The gift just comes bundled with the challenge of dealing with the associated excess, exacerbated by the unfortunate way our information economy has developed to focus on exploiting our attention rather than serving us.

We can all learn to maximize the potential and minimize the negative from this reality. Those who do that best will succeed, not just for themselves, but in all their endeavors, which for some include saving humanity from itself.

Humans by their intrinsic nature will always seek to learn, to grow, to invent, to progress. Faster flows of information accelerate that process. The more we share, the more we can become. It is up to each of us to make the most of the incredible abundance and potential of the information resources we have. The answer is to get better at this, not to limit the pace of development of what author Ramez Naam calls "the infinite resource": ideas.[10]

Network society thinker and educator Clay Shirky concurs. "I'm just so impatient with the argument that the world should be slowed down to help people who aren't smart enough to understand what's going on," he says.[11]

Having read this book, you are now better equipped to thrive on information abundance and make the most of the extraordinary times we live in, defined by acceleration and exponential growth. Over to you. You are the one who will make the choices, do the work, and develop the capabilities required to thrive in these intensely exciting times of boundless opportunity.

Keep in Touch!

Thank you so much for staying the course through this book! My dearest hope is that it has proved valuable to you. It is of course up to you to apply what I have offered to make it useful. My job has been to provide you with as useful tools, approaches, and perspectives as I possibly can.

My intention was to keep this book compact and easy to digest, despite the vast scope of the topic. If you wish to go beyond what I've been able to pack into this book, my team and I have compiled a wealth of resources to assist you on the book website. It contains:

- All the exercises from this book for you to download and print.
- Every one of the interviews I did for this book in my podcast *Thriving on Overload*, packed with incredible insights (far more than I could include in this book!) from the likes of author Nir Eyal, publisher Tim O'Reilly, futurist Cathy Hackl, venture capitalist Gary Swart, technology columnist Christopher Mims, and dozens of other highly inspiring guests.
- A highly interactive online course that guides you through creating a detailed Personal Information Plan to help you thrive.

- Frameworks, tools, productivity hacks, reviews of software tools, and other useful content.
- Links to the online Thriving on Overload communities where you can learn from others who share their insights and tips on how to thrive on overload, and where I hang out (say hi!).

Simply go to thrivingonoverload.com.

EXERCISES

Your Action Plan

In summary, what actions will you take to enable you to thrive on overload?

	What Actions Will You Take to Thrive on Overload?
Immediate	
Medium-term	
Long-term	

RESOURCES FOR THRIVING

There are many valuable resources for us to draw on in our journey to thriving. Here is a selection of further avenues to pursue beyond the starting point provided by this book.

Further Reading

If you have been inspired to go deeper than what I've been able to fit into these pages, here is a collection of wonderful books and articles to consider.

Introduction
The Information by James Gleick
> A masterful overview of the history and present of how we think about information

Chapter 1
Zen and the Art of Making a Living by Laurence Boldt
> A beautiful reflection on how to find your place in the world, filled with practical exercises

The News by Alain de Botton
> A philosophical reflection on our relationship to news

Essentialism by Greg McKeown
An inspiring paean to doing only what is essential

Chapter 2
WTF by Tim O'Reilly
O'Reilly on how he creates maps to make sense of the progress
of technology

How to Take Smart Notes by Sönke Ahrens
A practical book that has popularized the Zettelkasten method
of connected note-taking

The Pyramid Principle by Barbara Minto
Used extensively by consultants to structure their thinking

Gödel Escher Bach by Douglas Hofstadter
A mind-expanding tome exploring the deepest foundations of
thought

Systems Thinking Tools: A User's Guide by Daniel H. Kim
(thesystemsthinker.com/systems-thinking-tools-a-users-reference
-guide/)
An excellent compact introduction to systems thinking and
systems diagrams

Thinking in Systems: A Primer by Donella Meadows
A seminal text by one of the foundational thinkers in the field

Chapter 3
The Organized Mind by Daniel Levitin
A cognitive approach to overload focusing on organizing
information in your life

Calling Bullshit by Jevin West and Carl Bergstrom
An engaging tour through useful tools and approaches to
distinguish what is worthy of your attention

Thinking, Fast and Slow by Daniel Kahneman
Distills extensive research into the neurology of cognitive biases and the implications

Chapter 4
Deep Work by Cal Newport
A strong case and practical guidance for highly focused, completely undistracted work; a number of Newport's other books, including *The Time-Block Planner* and *A World Without Email*, are also relevant and useful

Indistractable by Nir Eyal
Practical guidance on how to move from distraction to traction

Focus by Daniel Goleman
An engaging exploration of the value and practice of focused attention

How to Read a Book by Mortimer Adler
The classic text on how to get value from reading, highlighting the need for flexibility

Breakthrough Rapid Reading by Peter Kump
A solid example of the many books available on classic speed-reading techniques

The Distracted Mind by Adam Gazzaley and Larry Rosen
The science of our brains' response to pervasive distractions and our potential responses

Chapter 5
The Eureka Factor by John Kounios and Mark Beeman
Leading neuroscientists share lessons learned from studying the nature of insight

Think Again by Adam Grant
> A strong, deeply grounded case for being open to changing your mind

Impro by Keith Johnstone
> A life-changing introduction to the philosophy and practice of improvisational theater

Thinking in Bets by Annie Duke
> Useful lessons in good decision-making and thinking derived from poker

A Tradecraft Primer: Structured Analytic Techniques for Improving Intelligence Analysis by Center for the Study of Intelligence
> A summary of useful techniques for better thinking provided by the US intelligence community

Consilience by Edward O. Wilson
> A landmark text on how synthesis lies at the heart of science, progress, and humanity

Mind and Nature by Gregory Bateson
> A beautiful book expressing foundational thinking on synthesis and systems thinking

Chapter 6
The Extended Mind by Annie Murphy Paul
> How we can think beyond our brains, in our bodies, surroundings, and relationships

Superminds by Thomas Malone
> How groups of humans and computers can together achieve superior intelligence

Content

Here are other kinds of resources to improve your information capabilities.

Podcasts

Thriving on Overload (thrivingonoverload.com/episodes)
    All the interviews done for this book, plus many more with inspiring information masters

Knowledge Project (fs.blog)
    Shane Parrish's *Knowledge Project* podcast and website overlaps substantially with the themes of this book

The Tim Ferriss Show (tim.blog)
    Tim's interviews regularly include details of his fascinating guests' information habits

Huberman Lab (hubermanlab.com)
    Many episodes of Stanford University professor Andrew Huberman's podcasts deal with the neuroscience of improving attention

Training and Education

Calling Bullshit (callingbullshit.org)
    A set of free resources from the famous University of Washington course

Media LIT: Overcoming Information Overload (edx.org/course /media-lit-overcoming-information-overload)
    A free online course created by pioneering journalist Dan Gillmor

Technology and Tools

This section provides a representative compilation of apps and technology tools you may find useful. There are dozens more tools of equal quality to those included here, so don't limit yourself to what you find on this list—seek the best ones for you!

Feed Readers
Three of the most commonly used RSS readers, each with distinctive features including granular filtering and recommendations:

Feedly (feedly.com)

Inoreader (inoreader.com)

NewsBlur (newsblur.com)

Two of the more prominent app-based email newsletter aggregators:

Stoop (stoopinbox.com)

Slick Inbox (slickinbox.com)

Algorithmic Aggregators
A handful of general-purpose and industry-specific aggregators beyond those provided by the major technology companies:

Flipboard (flipboard.com)
   A popular platform for curated and personalized content

News360 (news360.com)
   An app-based aggregator that refines results based on user feedback

Hacker News (news.ycombinator.com)
   The current reference aggregator for the startup community

Techmeme (techmeme.com)

Mediagazer (mediagazer.com)

Memeorandum (memeorandum.com)
   Gabe Rivera's social-signal-driven aggregators provide very
   useful single-stop views of the latest in technology, media, and
   US politics and society

Reading Apps
These apps offer a variety of features, including read-it-later,
formatting for reading, text-to-audio, and surfacing relevant content:

Pocket (getpocket.com)
   A well-established platform for bookmarking and content
   sharing

Matter (getmatter.app)
   A next-generation reading app for enhanced reading and
   curated discovery

Instapaper (instapaper.com)
   A cross-platform read-it-later application

Connected Note-Taking Apps
Each of these platforms has enthusiastic advocates. Preferences are
highly personal, depending on your thinking styles.

Roam (roamresearch.com)
   A popular online platform for making and connecting notes

Obsidian (obsidian.md)
   An open-source app-based alternative to Roam

TheBrain (thebrain.com)
   The original connected note-taking app, still widely used

Notion (notion.so)
   Not explicitly designed for connecting notes; however, it can
   be used this way

Focus Apps
There are dozens of focus apps for both computers and phones.
Here is a small selection representing different categories:

Cold Turkey (getcoldturkey.com)
A desktop app that schedules blocks of time and limits access
to selected content and apps

Freedom (freedom.to)
Blocks distractions across all your devices

Focusmate (focusmate.com)
Get paired with a partner to keep you accountable to
remaining focused for a period

Clockwise (getclockwise.com)
Designed to optimize your calendar to free up timeblocks for
focused attention

Space (findyourphonelifebalance.com)
Smartphone app to track your usage, set goals, and
improve habits

News Feed Eradicator
Chrome and Firefox extension that replaces the newsfeed of a
variety of social media sites with an inspiring quote

Writing Apps
Some apps are dedicated to writing, assisting by eliminating
distractions.

FocusWriter (gottcode.org/focuswriter/)
A free distraction-free word processor

Typora (typora.io)
A multifeatured app for writing and reading using markdown
for plaintext formatting

ACKNOWLEDGMENTS

This book owes its existence to my exceptional agent Jim Levine. I had spent an inordinate amount of time on a lengthy proposal for a sprawling book on how to think about and create the future, and I managed to get it into the hands of a few top literary agents. All of them told me they couldn't sell it. However, Jim read the proposal carefully, told me I was trying to cram three or four books into one, and said that if I took one of the chapters in the proposed book, titled "Thriving on Overload," and made that into a book, he was sure he could find a good publisher.

I am deeply grateful that Jim recognized that potential. I have long intended to write this book, having first started developing the ideas in 1997 and registering the domain thrivingonoverload .com in 2009. However, I thought I would get to it later in my writing career. But Jim was spot on: this is the right time to write this book, and I am extremely glad to have written this book rather than the one I proposed. Big thanks are also due to my old friend Tom Stewart, who introduced me to Jim.

I was aided immensely by Ann Graham, who worked with me on both book proposals as well as providing her usual unsparing, razor-sharp feedback on a draft of the entire book to help whip it into shape.

It has been a pleasure working with Casey Ebro, Scott Sewell, Donya Dickerson, Jonathan Sperling, and the rest of the talented team at McGraw Hill. Their experience and perspective have helped make the book immeasurably better. Kevin Commins provided valuable feedback during final development of the manuscript. Thank you to Michele Matrisciani, who shared useful perspectives as I prepared the manuscript. Alison Shurtz's copyedit of the book was thorough and perceptive. Steve Straus did an excellent job on the book production and was a pleasure to work with.

It has been a great pleasure working with Mark Fortier, Rebecca Proulx, and the rest of the team at Fortier PR in helping the book be found by those who might find it useful. Their collaborative approach was an excellent fit.

I knew that the people I interviewed for the book would have incredible insights to share, many of which I would not be able to fit into the book, so I recorded my interviews as the *Thriving on Overload* podcast series. Deep thanks for their time and illuminating perspectives from all those I was able to interview before I had to submit the manuscript: Tim O'Reilly, Cathy Hackl, Nir Eyal, Tom Stewart, Jerry Michalski, Robert Scoble, Leslie Shannon, Brett King, Harold Jarche, Annalie Killian, Dan Gillmor, R "Ray" Wang, Robin Athey, Michell Zappa, Marshall Kirkpatrick, Gary Swart, Madeline Ashby, and Christopher Mims. I was not able to quote everyone directly in the book, but they all contributed to the final product.

Other people whose expertise and provocative perspectives added to the book include Bernard Balleine, Napier Collyns, Chris Dancy, Graham Dawson, Peta Estens, Oliver Freeman, Christine Gallagher, Josie Gibson, Terri Griffith, John Hagel, Brett King, David Kenney, Gerd Leonhard, Chris Meyer, Tony Morriss, Ramez Naam, Charis Palmer, Mark Pesce, Howard Rheingold, Euan Semple, Brian Solis, Mike Walsh, and Richard Watson. Forgive me if I have overlooked anyone from the many who have contributed to my thinking on the topic, of which there have been probably hundreds over the past two decades.

It was a pleasure to work once again with Daniil Alexandrov on the diagram design in what is now our third book collaboration over a period of more than a decade. Working with Sam Barton, Brian Sowards, and Gio Kakhiani on the *Thriving on Overload* course and platform has been exciting and rewarding. I'm looking forward to seeing what our project becomes.

There have been many who have played vital roles in supporting my ventures run in parallel to writing this book. To all the Advanced Human Technologies Group team, especially Jenna Owsianik, thank you for driving things forward while my attention was pulled elsewhere. Everything good about Bondi Innovation Hub before its untimely death by Covid-19, and for Bondi Innovation thereafter, was driven by the inspiring energy of Julia Dominguez, Nicole McKay, David Warwick, the Hub residents, and the many others involved.

Through the course of writing this book it has been a massive boon to be working with the highly talented Jay Kemp and Tanja Markovic of Provoke Management for all my keynote speaking and corporate engagements. It is a pleasure to work with you, and I look forward to our continued success together.

Thank you to Elena for being with me. I am blessed to have you in my life.

My daughters, Leda and Phoebe, are at the heart of my life; they are precious, delightful, and inspiring. Thank you so much to both of you for your understanding as I have taken so much time to work on the book, and thank you for being your marvelous selves. I love you so much!

NOTES

Introduction

1. James Gleick, *The Information: A History, a Theory, a Flood* (Pantheon, 2011), 8.
2. Alvin Toffler, *Future Shock* (Random House, 1970), 355.
3. Bertram M. Gross, *The Managing of Organizations* (The Free Press of Glencoe, 1964).
4. Daisuke Wakabayashi, "Google Dominates Thanks to an Unrivaled View of the Web," *New York Times*, December 14, 2000, https://www.nytimes.com/2020/12/14/technology/how-google-dominates.html; and https://www.internetworldstats.com/stats.htm.
5. Information from figures in Dylan Tweney, "Here Comes the Zettabyte Age," *Wired*, April 30, 2010, https://www.wired.com/2010/04/here-comes-the-zettabyte-age/; and UNCTAD, *Digital Economy Report 2021*, August 2021, 17, https://unctad.org/system/files/official-document/der2021_en.pdf.
6. Author's calculations.
7. Rani Molla, "Tech Companies Tried to Help Us Spend Less Time on Our Phones. It Didn't Work," *Vox*, January 6, 2020, https://www.vox.com/recode/2020/1/6/21048116/tech-companies-time-well-spent-mobile-phone-usage-data.
8. Andrew Perrin and Sara Atske, "About Three-in-Ten U.S. Adults Say They Are 'Almost Constantly' Online," *Pew Research Center*, March 26, 2021, https://www.pewresearch.org/fact-tank/2021/03/26/about-three-in-ten-u-s-adults-say-they-are-almost-constantly-online/.
9. Jeffrey Gottfried, "Americans' News Fatigue Isn't Going Away—About Two-Thirds Still Feel Worn Out," *Pew Research Center*, February 26,

2020, https://www.pewresearch.org/fact-tank/2020/02/26/almost-seven-in-ten-americans-have-news-fatigue-more-among-republicans/.

10. Carl Sagan, "The Burden of Skeptisicm," *Skeptical Inquirer* 12, Fall 1987, https://www.arvindguptatoys.com/arvindgupta/sagan-skeptism.pdf.

11. Iain McGilchrist, *The Master and His Emissary: The Divided Brain and the Making of the Western World* (Yale University Press, 2012).

Chapter 1

1. Yuval Noah Harari, *21 Lessons for the 21st Century* (Random House, 2018), ix.

2. Andrew Sih, "Optimal Behavior: Can Foragers Balance Two Conflicting Demands?" *Science* 210 (4473), 1041–1043, https://doi.org/10.1126/science.210.4473.1041.

3. Peter Pirolli and Stuart Card, "Information Foraging in Information Access Environments," *Proceedings of the SIGCHI Conference on Human Factors in Computing Systems*—CHI '95, May 1995, 51–59, https://doi.org/10.1145/223904.223911.

4. OECD, Obesity Update 2017, https://www.oecd.org/els/health-systems/Obesity-Update-2017.pdf.

5. Herminia Ibarra, *Working Identity* (Harvard Business Review Press, 2004), 96.

6. Original source unknown; taken from Brené Brown, *Braving the Wilderness: The Quest for True Belonging and the Courage to Stand Alone* (Random House, 2017), 40.

7. Tim Ferriss (host), "Jacqueline Novogratz on Building Acumen, How to (Actually) Change the World, Speaking Your Truth, and the Incredible Power of 'Dumb' Questions (#512)," *The Tim Ferriss Show*, May 3, 2021, https://tim.blog/2021/05/04/jacqueline-novogratz/; and "Interview: Building a World Based on Dignity," *Leaders* 44, no. 3 (July, August, September 2021), 110–112, http://www.leadersmag.com/issues/2021.3_Jul/ROB/LEADERS-Jacqueline-Novogratz-Acumen.html.

8. "Jacqueline Novogratz - Gettysburg College Commencement 2012," YouTube, Gettysburg College channel, 7:29, https://www.youtube.com/watch?v=fSAxFpfodZ8.

9. Jonathan M. Spector, Rosemary S. Harrison, and Mark C. Fishman, "Fundamental Science Behind Today's Important Medicines," *Science Translational Medicine* 10, no. 438, https://doi.org/10.1126/scitranslmed.aaq1787.

10. Alyson Shontell, "A Hot-Shot Magazine Editor and a Tijuana Teenager Met Online and Made $5 Million Building Drones," *Business Insider*, December 13, 2014, https://www.businessinsider.com/how-3d-robotics -founders-chris-anderson-and-jordi-munoz-met-2014-12.

11. Regan Morris, "The Mexican Immigrant Who Set up a Global Drone Firm," BBC, February 23, 2015, https://www.bbc.com/news/business -31356080.

12. Patrick Collison, "Bookshelf," *Patrick Collison* (website), https:// patrickcollison.com/bookshelf.

13. Robert Greene (@robertgreene), "The future belongs to those who learn more skills and combine them in creative ways." Twitter, August 15, 2018, https://twitter.com/robertgreene/status/1029444554783698946.

14. Ashlee Vance, "This Tech Bubble Is Different," *Bloomberg Businessweek*, April 14, 2011, http://www.bloomberg.com/news/articles/2011-04-14 /this-tech-bubble-is-different.

15. Cayla Sharp and Angelica Pan, "Jeff Hammerbacher—From Data Science to Biomedicine," *Gradient Dissident*, https://wandb.ai/wandb _fc/gradient-dissent/reports/Jeff-Hammerbacher-From-data-science-to -biomedicine--Vmlldzo4NjQzMzk.

16. Marshall McLuhan, *The Medium Is the Massage: An Inventory of Effects* (Gingko Press, 2001), 70.

17. Alain de Botton, "How to Stop News from Ruining Our Lives," CNN, March 7, 2014, https://edition.cnn.com/2014/03/07/opinion/news -ruins-lives-opinion/index.html.

18. Thomas Baekdel (@baekdal), "I will try to write a more detailed article about this, but the more you look at this, the more you realize that the way we do news today is seriously harmful to people's mental health." *Twitter*, September 29, 2021, https://twitter.com/baekdal /status/1443098699501084674.

19. Chris Dancy, *Don't Unplug: How Technology Saved My Life and Can Save Yours* (St. Martin's Press, 2018), 155–172, 243.

20. Lydia Moynihan, "Goldman CEO Defends DJ'ing Habit, Admits Barry Manilow a 'Guilty Pleasure'," *New York Post*, December 3, 2021, https://nypost.com/2021/12/03/goldman-ceo-defends-djing-habit -admits-barry-manilow-a-guilty-pleasure/.

Chapter 2

1. M. McLuhan, *Counterblast* (McClelland and Stewart, 1969), 132.

2. Ross Dawson, host, "Jerry Michalski on Collecting, Connecting, and Curating Two Decades Worth of Information (Ep5)," *Thriving on*

Overload (podcast), https://thrivingonoverload.com/jerry-michalski
-on-collecting-connecting-and-curating-two-decades-worth-of
-information-ep5/.

3. Max Chafkin, "The Oracle of Silicon Valley," *Inc.*, May 1, 2010, https://
www.inc.com/magazine/20100501/the-oracle-of-silicon-valley.html.

4. Tim O'Reilly, *WTF: What's the Future and Why It's Up to Us* (Harper
Business, October 2017), 3.

5. Ross Dawson, host, "Tim O'Reilly on Noticing Things Other People
Don't Notice, the Value of Soft Focus, Framing Open Source and Web
2.0, and Patience in Building Narratives (Ep1)," *Thriving on Overload*
(podcast), December 13, 2021, https://thrivingonoverload.com/tim
-oreilly-noticing-soft-focus-open-source-web-2-0/.

6. O'Reilly, *Thriving on Overload*.

7. O'Reilly, *WTF*, 35.

8. Ross Dawson, *Developing Knowledge-Based Client Relationships*, 2nd ed.
(Butterworth Heinemann, 2005), 16.

9. Herbert A. Simon, *Models of My Life* (MIT Press Academic, 1996), 5.

10. Simon, *Models of My Life*, 55–56.

11. Anders Ericsson, *Peak: Secrets from the New Science of Expertise* (Harp-
erOne, 2016), loc. 1941 of 6116, Kindle.

12. Ericsson, *Peak*, loc. 1215 of 6116, Kindle.

13. See Logan Fiorella and Richard E. Mayer, "Spontaneous Spatial Strategy Use in Learning from Scientific Text," *Contemporary Educational
Psychology* 49, April 2017: 66–79; and Chei-Chang Chiou, "The Effect
of Concept Mapping on Students' Learning Achievements and Interests," *Innovations in Education and Teaching International* 45, no. 4
(2008).

14. The terms "data visualization" and "information visualization" are
often used interchangeably. The latter tends to refer to more sophisticated representations, often explicitly supporting decisions.

15. Ross Dawson (host), "Gary Swart on Achieving Balance, Prioritization
Factors, Filtering by Relationships, and Using Frameworks (Ep15)," *Thriving on Overload* (podcast), https://thrivingonoverload.com/gary-swart
-achieving-balance-prioritization-factors-filtering-relationships-using
-frameworks-ep15/.

16. Elon Musk, "Ask Me Anything (AMA)," Reddit, January 5, 2015, https://
www.reddit.com/r/IAmA/comments/2rgsan/i_am_elon_musk_ceocto
_of_a_rocket_company_ama/.

17. Emma Sinclair, "The First Female Grads of Harvard Business School
Led the Way for All of Us," *The Telegraph*, May 17, 2016, https://

web.archive.org/web/20130315040551/https://www.telegraph.co.uk
/women/womens-business/9925405/The-first-female-grads-of-Harvard
-Business-School-led-the-way-for-all-of-us.html.

18. Barbara Minto, *The Minto Pyramid Principle: Logic in Thinking and Writing* (Minto International, 1996), 9.
19. George A. Miller, "The Magic Number Seven, Plus or Minus Two: Some Limits on Our Capacity for Processing Information," *Psychological Review* 63 (1956), 91–97.
20. William G. Chase and Herbert A. Simon, "Perception in Chess," *Cognitive Psychology* 4, no. 1 (January 1973), 55–81.
21. Douglas Hofstadter, *Gödel Escher Bach: An Eternal Golden Braid* (Basic Books, 1979).
22. Thomas Lask, "Publishing: A Heavy Price for a Heavy Book," *New York Times*, October 5, 1979, Section C, p. 30, https://www.nytimes.com /1979/10/05/archives/publishing-a-heavy-price-for-a-heavy-book.html.
23. Tony Buzan with Barry Buzan, *The Mind Map Book: Radiant Thinking; The Major Development in Human Thought*, rev. ed. (BBC Books, 1995).
24. Albert-László Barabási, *Linked: How Everything Is Connected to Everything Else and What It Means for Business, Science, and Everyday Life* (Plume, 2003).
25. The Human Connectome Project is one of the primary projects in this space. The underlying thinking has been well expressed by one of the project's founders in Olaf Sporns, *Networks of the Brain* (MIT Press, 2010).
26. Carla A. Shatz, "The Developing Brain," *Scientific American* 267, no. 3, Special Issue: Mind and Brain (September 1992), 60–67, https://www .jstor.org/stable/24939213.
27. George Lakoff, *Women, Fire, and Dangerous Things: What Categories Reveal About the Mind* (University of Chicago Press, 1990).
28. David Weinberger, *Everything Is Miscellaneous: The Power of the New Digital Disorder* (Henry Holt & Company, 2007).
29. Tim Berners-Lee, *Information Management: A Proposal*, March 1989, May 1990, http://cds.cern.ch/record/369245/files/dd-89-001.pdf.
30. See John Hagel III, John Seely Brown, and Lang Davison, "The New Organization Model: Learning at Scale," *Harvard Business Review*, March 11, 2009; and John Hagel III and John Seely Brown, "Great Businesses Scale Their Learning, Not Just Their Operations," *Harvard Business Review*, June 7, 2017.
31. Lawrence M. Fisher, "The Prophet of Unintended Consequences," *Strategy+Business*, no. 40, August 26, 2005, https://www.strategy -business.com/article/05308.

32. "Timeline of Instagram," *Wikipedia*, https://en.wikipedia.org/wiki /Timeline_of_Instagram.

33. Brad Stone, *The Everything Store: Jeff Bezos and the Age of Amazon* (Little Brown, 2013), 82; diagram structure retrieved from https://jobs-us -east.amazon.com/en/landing_pages/about-amazon.

34. Brenda Barbosa, "Billionaire Richard Branson Does This at Every Meeting. Here's Why You Should Do It Too," *Inc.*, June 9, 2017, https:// www.inc.com/brenda-barbosa/the-habit-billionaire-richard-branson -swears-by-and-how-you-can-cultivate-it-to.html.

35. Rudolf Stichweh, "Luhmann, Niklas (1927–98)," *International Encyclopedia of the Social & Behavioral Sciences*, 2nd ed., 2015: 382–389, https://doi.org/10.1016/B978-0-08-097086-8.61080-2.

36. Staffan Müller-Wille and Isabelle Charmantier, "Natural History and Information Overload: The Case of Linnaeus," *Studies in History and Philosophy of Science Part C: Studies in History and Philosophy of Biological and Biomedical Sciences* 43, no. 1, (March 2012), 4–15, https://doi .org/10.1016/j.shpsc.2011.10.021.

37. R. U. Sirius, "The Psychedelic Inspiration for Hypercard," *Mondo 2000*, http://www.mondo2000.com/2018/06/18/the-inspiration-for-hypercard/.

38. Brad Feld, "Roam: My New Favorite Software Product," *Brad Feld* (blog), November 2, 2020, https://feld.com/archives/2020/11/roam-my -new-favorite-software-product/.

39. John F. Nestojko, Dung C. Bui, Nate Kornell, and Elizabeth Ligon Bjork, "Expecting to Teach Enhances Learning and Organization of Knowledge in Free Recall of Text Passages," *Memory & Cognition* 42, May 21, 2014, 1038–1048, https://doi.org/10.3758/s13421-014-0416-z.

40. Warren Buffett, Whitney Tilson (ed.), "Three Lectures by Warren Buffett to Notre Dame Faculty, MBA Students and Undergraduate Students," Spring 1991,23, http://www.tilsonfunds.com/BuffettNotreDame.pdf.

41. Paul Graham, "The Age of the Essay," *Paul Graham* (blog), http://www .paulgraham.com/essay.html.

42. Jessica Stillman, "The Return of Writing," *Inc.*, December 7, 2012, https://www.inc.com/jessica-stillman/the-return-of-writing.html.

43. This oft-quoted phrase was apparently originally stated by Danish politician Karl Kristian Steincke. See "It's Difficult to Make Predictions, Especially About the Future," *Quote Investigator*, October 20, 2013, https://quoteinvestigator.com/2013/10/20/no-predict/.

44. Catalin V. Buhusi, Sorinel A. Oprisan, and Mona Buhusi, "Biological and Cognitive Frameworks for a Mental Timeline," *Frontiers in Neuroscience*, June 11, 2018, https://doi.org/10.3389/fnins.2018.00377.

45. Ross Dawson, "Further Explanation and Answers to 6 Questions on the Newspaper Extinction Timeline After One Million Views," *Ross Dawson* (blog), November 18, 2010, https://rossdawson.com/further_explana/.

46. 24:7 "Ross Dawson," *Australian Financial Review BOSS* magazine, December 2013.

47. Ross Dawson, "Review of the Newspaper Extinction Timeline: What We Got Wrong and the Future of News from Here," *Ross Dawson* (blog), December 15, 2017, https://rossdawson.com/review-newspaper-extinction-timeline-got-wrong-future-news/.

48. Personal conversation.

49. Paul J.H. Schoemaker, George S. Day, and Scott A. Snyder, "Integrating Organizational Networks, Weak Signals, Strategic Radars and Scenario Planning," *Technological Forecasting and Social Change* 80, no. 4: 815–824, https://doi.org/10.1016/j.techfore.2012.10.020.

50. All my public visual frameworks are available at https://rossdawson.com/frameworks.

51. High-resolution color version available at https://rossdawson.com/frameworks/humans-in-the-future-of-work/.

52. Ross Dawson, "Future of Media Strategic Framework," *Ross Dawson*, June 8, 2006, https://rossdawson.com/frameworks/future-of-media-framework/.

Chapter 3

1. Sagan, "The Burden of Skepticism."

2. Jimmy Soni and Rob Goodman, "A Man in a Hurry: Claude Shannon's New York Years" *IEEE Spectrum*, July 12, 2017, https://spectrum.ieee.org/a-man-in-a-hurry-claude-shannons-new-york-years.

3. Nassim Nicholas Taleb, *Antifragile: Things That Gain from Disorder* (Random House, 2012), 126.

4. Brad Feld, "Signal vs. Noise," *Brad Feld* (blog), February 27, 2011, https://feld.com/archives/2011/02/signal-vs-noise/.

5. These oft-quoted (though not necessarily accurate) figures originate from Tor Nørretranders, *The User Illusion: Cutting Consciousness Down to Size* (Penguin Book, 1999).

6. Aldous Huxley, *The Doors of Perception* (Chatto & Windus, 1954), 6.

7. Elif Isbell, Courtney Stevens, Eric Pakulak, Amanda Hampton Wray, Theodore A. Bell, and Helen J. Neville, "Neuroplasticity of Selective Attention," *Proceedings of the National Academy of Sciences*, August 2017, 114 (35), 9247–9254, https://doi.org10.1073/pnas.1707241114.

8. From the screenplay by Marguerite Duras for the classic film *Hiroshima, Mon Amour*, Alain Resnais, dir., 1959.

9. Karl-Erik Sveiby, "Transfer of Knowledge and the Information Processing Profession," *European Management Journal*, August 1996, 14 (4), 379–388, https://doi.org/10.1016/0263-2373(96)00025-4.

10. Elroy Boers, Mohammad H. Afzali, Nicola Newton, and Patricia Conrod, "Association of Screen Time and Depression in Adolescence," *JAMA Pediatrics*, 2019, 173 (9), 853–859, https://doi.org/10.1001/jamapediatrics.2019.1759.

11. Tiger Webb, " 'Doomscrolling' and 'Rona' Top Macquarie Dictionary Word of the Year Picks," *ABC News*, November 30, 2020, https://www.abc.net.au/news/2020-11-30/macquarie-dictionary-word-of-the-year-doomscrolling-rona/12928010.

12. Cass R. Sunstein and Richard Thaler, "The Two Friends Who Changed How We Think About How We Think," *New Yorker*, December 7, 2016, https://www.newyorker.com/books/page-turner/the-two-friends-who-changed-how-we-think-about-how-we-think.

13. Daniel Kahnemann, *Thinking, Fast and Slow* (Farrar, Straus and Giroux, 2011), 28.

14. Cade Metz, "Silicon Valley's Safe Space," *New York Times*, February 13, 2021, https://www.nytimes.com/2021/02/13/technology/slate-star-codex-rationalists.html.

15. Philip E. Tetlock and Dan Gardner, *Superforecasting: The Art and Science of Prediction* (Crown, 2010), 171.

16. John Kounios and Mark Beeman, *The Eureka Factor: AHA Moments, Creative Insight, and the Brain* (Random House, 2015), 41–42.

17. Nassim Nicholas Taleb, *The Bed of Procrustes: Philosophical and Practical Aphorisms* (Random House, 2010), 21.

18. Peter Kelley, "After Much Media Attention, UW Information School's 'Calling BS' Class Begins," *UW News*, March 28, 2017, https://www.washington.edu/news/2017/03/28/after-much-media-attention-uw-information-schools-calling-bs-class-begins/.

19. Carl T. Bergstrom and Jevin D. West, *Calling Bullshit: The Art of Scepticism in a Data-Driven World* (Allen Lane, 2020).

20. Retrieved from http://retractiondatabase.org/.

21. I can find no verified source for these oft-quoted words; however, the attitude and thinking that underlies this sentiment can be found in Gregory Bateson, *Mind and Nature: A Necessary Unity* (E.P Dutton, 1979), 65–88.

22. Ross Dawson, "List of the World's Top Female Futurists," *RossDawson. com*, https://rossdawson.com/list-of-the-worlds-top-female-futurists/.

23. Homero Gil de Zúñiga, Brian Weeks, and Alberto Ardèvol-Abreu, "Effects of the News-Finds-Me Perception in Communication: Social Media Use Implications for News Seeking and Learning About Politics," *Journal of Computer-Mediated Communication* 22, no. 3 (May 1, 2017), 105–123, https://doi.org/10.1111/jcc4.12185.

24. Ross Dawson, host, "Tim O'Reilly on Noticing Things Other People Don't Notice, the Value of Soft Focus, Framing Open Source and Web 2.0, and Patience in Building Narratives (Ep1)," *Thriving on Overload* (podcast), December 13, 2021, https://thrivingonoverload.com/tim -oreilly-noticing-soft-focus-open-source-web-2-0/.

25. Elisa Shearer, "More Than Eight-in-Ten Americans Get News from Digital Devices," *Pew Research Center*, January 12, 2021, https:// www.pewresearch.org/fact-tank/2021/01/12/more-than-eight-in-ten -americans-get-news-from-digital-devices/.

26. Shane Parrish (host), "Josh Wolfe: Inventing the Future," *The Knowledge Project* (podcast), Ep.50, https://fs.blog/knowledge-podcast/josh -wolfe/.

27. Ross Dawson (host), "R 'Ray' Wang on Constant Curation, Learning from Private Networks, Finding Temporal Patterns, and Seeing the Impact of Trends (Ep11)," *Thriving on Overload* (podcast), https:// thrivingonoverload.com/ray-wang-constant-curation-learning-private -networks-temporal-patterns-seeing-impact-trends-ep11/.

28. Fred Wilson, "Prioritizing Content Consumption," *AVC*, February 20, 2018, https://avc.com/2018/02/prioritizing-content-consumption/.

29. Scott Rosenberg, *Say Everything: How Blogging Began, What It's Becoming, and Why It Matters* (Three Rivers Press, 2010), 50.

30. Eric Nuzum, "The Story of the First Podcast Feed," *Podnews*, January 20, 2021, https://podnews.net/article/first-podcast-feed-history.

31. Ross Dawson (host), "Robert Scoble on How to Find the Latest News, How to Use Twitter for Insight, Finding the 20 People You Need to Follow, and the Value of Conversations (Ep6)," *Thriving on Overload* (podcast), https://thrivingonoverload.com/robert-scoble-on-how-to-find -the-latest-news-how-to-use-twitter-for-insight-finding-the-20-people -you-need-to-follow-and-the-value-of-conversations-ep6/.

32. Ross Dawson (host), "Harold Jarche on Personal Knowledge Mastery, the Seek, Sense, and Share Framework; Networked Learning, and Finding Different Perspectives (Ep9)," *Thriving on Overload* (podcast),

https://thrivingonoverload.com/harold-jarche-personal-knowledge
-mastery-seek-sense-share-framework-networked-learning/.

33. Ross Dawson (host), "Marshall Kirkpatrick on Source Selection, Connecting Ideas, Diverse Thinking, and Enabling Serendipity (Ep14)," *Thriving on Overload* (podcast), https://thrivingonoverload .com/marshall-kirkpatrick-source-selection-connecting-ideas-diverse -thinking-enabling-serendipity-ep14/.

34. Ross Dawson (host), "Leslie Shannon on Finding Nuggets, Storytelling for Synthesis, the Five Fs of Sensemaking, and Visual Filing (Ep7)," *Thriving on Overload* (podcast), https://thrivingonoverload.com/leslie -shannon-storytelling-synthesis-sensemaking-ep7/.

35. Kimiko de Freytas-Tamura, "What's Next for Humanity: Automation, New Morality and a 'Global Useless Class'," *New York Times*, March 29, 2018, https://www.nytimes.com/2018/03/19/world/europe/yuval -noah-harari-future-tech.html.

36. Amy Mitchell, Mark Jurkowitz, J. Baxter Oliphant, and Elisa Shearer, "Americans Who Mainly Get Their News on Social Media," *Pew Research Center*, https://www.pewresearch.org/journalism/2020/07 /30/americans-who-mainly-get-their-news-on-social-media-are-less -engaged-less-knowledgeable/.

37. David Ingram, "Emoji Reactions Were a Cute Addition to Facebook. They Became a Headache," *NBC News*, October 28, 2021, https:// www.nbcnews.com/tech/tech-news/emoji-reactions-cute-addition -facebook-became-headache-rcna3747.

38. Charlie Warzel, "Meet the Man Whose Site Mark Zuckerberg Reads Every Day," *CNBC*, March 22, 2017, https://www.cnbc.com/2017/03 /22/meet-the-man-whose-site-mark-zuckerberg-reads-every-day.html.

39. Noah Brier, "The Monday Media Diet with Taylor Lorenz," *Why Is This Interesting?* (substack), February 17, 2020, https://whyisthisinteresting .substack.com/p/why-is-this-interesting-the-monday-e36.

40. Susanne Dietrich, Ingo Hertrich, and Hermann Ackermann, "Training of Ultra-Fast Speech Comprehension Induces Functional Reorganiza-tion of the Central-Visual System in Late-Blind Humans," *Frontiers in Human Neuroscience* 7 (October 23, 2013), 701, https://doi.org/10.3389 /fnhum.2013.00701.

41. Jim Milliot, "Print Books Had a Huge Sales Year in 2021," *Publish-ers Weekly*, January 6, 2022, https://www.publishersweekly.com/pw /by-topic/industry-news/financial-reporting/article/88225-print-book -sales-rose-8-9-in-2021.html.

42. David M. Sanbonmatsu, David L. Strayer, Nathan Medeiros-Ward, and Jason M. Watson "Who Multi-Tasks and Why? Multi-Tasking Ability, Perceived Multi-Tasking Ability, Impulsivity, and Sensation Seeking" *PLoS ONE* 8, no. 1 (2013) https://doi.org/10.1371/journal.pone.0054402.

43. Tim Ferriss (host), "Maria Popova on Writing, Workflow, and Work-arounds (#39)," *The Tim Ferris Show* (podcast), https://tim.blog/2014/10/21/brain-pickings/.

44. Shane Parrish (host), "Marc Andreessen: Interview with an Icon," *The Knowledge Project* (podcast), Episode #129, https://fs.blog/knowledge-podcast/marc-andreessen/.

45. Shane Parrish (host), "When to Trust Your Gut: Michael Mauboussin on Intuition, Technology, and Making Better Decisions," *The Knowledge Project* (podcast), Episode #1, https://fs.blog/knowledge-podcast/michael-mauboussin/.

46. Richard Saul Wurman, *Information Anxiety* (Bantam Doubleday Dell Publishing Group, 1989), 5.

47. Richard Koch and Greg Lockwood, *Superconnect: How the Best Connections in Business and Life Are the Ones You Least Expect* (Abacus, 2010).

48. Alex Williams, "On the Tip of Creative Tongues," *New York Times*, October 2, 2009, https://www.nytimes.com/2009/10/04/fashion/04curate.html.

49. Ross Dawson, *Living Networks: Leading Your Company, Customers, and Partners in the Hyper-Connected Economy* (Financial Times/ Prentice Hall, 2002), v.

50. Ross Dawson, "If You Help Bring the Networks to Life . . . You Will Create Success for Yourself," *Ross Dawson* (blog), August 4, 2021, https://rossdawson.com/if-you-help-bring-the-networks-to-life-you-will-create-success-for-yourself/.

51. Cal Newport, *Deep Work: Rules for Focused Success in a Distracted World* (Grand Central Publishing, 2016), 246.

Chapter 4

1. Oliver Burkeman, *Four Thousand Weeks: Time Management for Mortals* (Farrar, Straus and Giroux, 2021), 61.

2. Trevor Wheelwright, "Cell Phone Behavior in 2021: How Obsessed Are We?" *Reviews.org*, April 21, 2021, https://www.reviews.org/mobile/cell-phone-addiction/.

3. See Eyal Ophir, Clifford Nass, and Anthony D. Wagner, "Cognitive Control in Media Multitaskers," *Proceedings of the National Academy*

of Sciences 106, no. 37 (2009): 15583–87, https://doi.org/10.1073/pnas
.0903620106; and David M. Sanbonmatsu, David L. Strayer, Nathan
Medeiros-Ward, and Jason M. Watson, "Who Multi-Tasks and Why?
Multi-Tasking Ability, Perceived Multi-Tasking Ability, Impulsivity,
and Sensation Seeking," *PLoS ONE* 8, no. 1 (2013), https://doi.org/10
.1371/journal.pone.0054402.

4. Tim Ferriss (host), "Dr. Martine Rothblatt—A Masterclass on Asking
   Better Questions and Peering into the Future (#487)," *The Tim Ferriss Show* (podcast), December 16, 2020, https://tim.blog/2020/12/16
   /martine-rothblatt/.

5. Famous Speed Readers, *Iris*, May 7, 2008, https://irisreading.com
   /famous-speed-readers/.

6. Famous Speed Readers, *Iris*.

7. Nir Eyal, *Thriving on Overload*; Marina Gorbis, *The Tim Ferriss Show*.

8. Alex Barker, "The Surprising 'Superpower' Billionaires Want That
   You May Already Have," *Entrepreneur*, July 27, 2015, https://www
   .entrepreneur.com/article/247434.

9. Marcus E. Raichle and Abraham Z. Snyder, "A Default Mode of Brain
   Function: A Brief History of an Evolving Idea," *NeuroImage* 37, no. 4
   (2007): 1083–90, https://doi.org/10.1016/j.neuroimage.2007.02.041.

10. Jeff Weiner, "The Importance of Scheduling Nothing," *LinkedIn*,
    April 14, 2013, https://www.linkedin.com/pulse/20130403215758
    -22330283-the-importance-of-scheduling-nothing/.

11. Tim Ferris (host), "Michael Lewis—Inside the Mind of the Iconic
    Writer (#427)," *The Tim Ferris Show* (podcast), May 14, 2020, https://
    tim.blog/2020/05/14/michael-lewis-transcript/.

12. Nick Douglas, "I'm Quantitative Futurist Amy Webb, and This Is
    How I Work," *Lifehacker,* July 25, 2018, https://lifehacker.com/im
    -quantitative-futurist-amy-webb-and-this-is-how-i-wo-1826957435.

13. Jessica Wapner, "Vision and Breathing May Be the Secrets to Sur-
    viving 2020," *Scientific American*, November 16, 2020, https://www
    .scientificamerican.com/article/vision-and-breathing-may-be-the
    -secrets-to-surviving-2020/.

14. Ezra Wegbreit, Satoru Suzuki, Marcia Grabowecky, John Kounios, and
    Mark Beeman, "Visual Attention Modulates Insight Versus Analytic
    Solving of Verbal Problems," *Journal of Problem Solving*, 4, no. 2 (2012),
    94–115, https://doi.org/10.7771/1932-6246.1127.

15. John Ezard, "Serendipity Is Our Favourite Word," *The Guardian*, Sep-
    tember 19, 2000, https://www.theguardian.com/uk/2000/sep/19/books
    .booksnews.

16. Ross Dawson, "Creating Enhanced Serendipity," *Ross Dawson* (blog), https://rossdawson.com/creating_enhanc/.

17. Shane Parrish (host), "Sanjay Bakshi: A Multi-Disciplinary Approach to Learning," *The Knowledge Project* (podcast), Ep. #3, https://fs.blog /knowledge-podcast/sanjay-bakshi/.

18. Rebecca A. Clay, "Green Is Good for You," *American Psychological Association* 32, no. 4 (April 2001), https://www.apa.org/monitor/apr01 /greengood.html.

19. Stephen Kaplan, "The Restorative Benefits of Nature: Toward an Integrative Framework," *Journal of Environmental Psychology* 15, no. 3 (1995), 169–182, https://doi.org/10.1016/0272-4944(95)90001-2.

20. Stephen Kaplan and Marc G. Berman, "Directed Attention as a Common Resource for Executive Functioning and Self-Regulation," *Perspectives on Psychological Science* 5, no. 1 (January 1, 2010), 43–57, https://doi.org/10.1177/1745691609356784.

21. Tim Ferriss (host), "Seth Godin on How to Say 'No,' Market Like a Professional, and Win at Life (#343)," *The Tim Ferriss Show* (podcast), November 1, 2018, https://tim.blog/2018/11/01/seth-godin-this-is -marketing/.

22. Sriram Krishnan, "Daniel Ek," *The Observer Effect*, October 4, 2020, https://www.theobservereffect.org/daniel.html.

23. Jacques Taillard, Pierre Philip, and Bernard Bioulac, "Morningness/ Eveningness and the Need for Sleep," *Journal of Sleep Research* 8, no. 4 (December 1999), 291–295, https://doi.org/10.1046/j.1365-2869.1999 .00176.x.

24. Steve Pavlina, "Timeboxing," *Steve Pavlina* (blog), October 18, 2004, https://stevepavlina.com/blog/2004/10/timeboxing/.

25. Nir Eyal, "Timeboxing: The Simple Productivity System You're Not Using," *Nir Eyal* (blog), https://www.nirandfar.com/timeboxing/.

26. Weiner, *LinkedIn*.

27. Andy Orin, "I'm Max Levchin, CEO of Affirm and Co-Founder of PayPal, and This Is How I Work," *Lifehacker*, January 25, 2017, https:// lifehacker.com/im-max-levchin-ceo-of-affirm-and-co-founder-of -paypal-1791439921.

28. Wheelright, "Cell Phone Behavior."

29. Mark Abadi, "Disney CEO Bob Iger Wakes Up at 4:15 Every Morning and Enacts a Technology 'Firewall' Until After His Workout," *Business Insider*, October 11, 2018, https://www.businessinsider.com/disney-bob -iger-morning-routine-2018-10.

30. Jen Doll, "Brian Stelter: What I Read," *The Wire*, February 16, 2012, https://web.archive.org/web/20150307050553/http://www.thewire.com/business/2012/02/brian-stelter-what-i-read/48774.

31. Originally reported in Akira Kasamatsu and Tomio Hirai, *Psychiatry and Clinical Neurosciences* 20, no. 4 (December 1966), 315–336, https://doi.org/10.1111/j.1440-1819.1966.tb02646.x, though more recent studies have shown mixed results on habituation in practiced meditators, such as Elena Antonova, Paul Chadwick, and Veena Kumari, "More Meditation, Less Habituation? The Effect of Mindfulness Practice on the Acoustic Startle Reflex," *PLOS One* 10 (7): e0133099, May 6, 2015, https://doi.org/10.1371/journal.pone.0133099.

32. Victor Fic, "Zen and the Real World," *The Japan International Journal* 1, no. 5 (October 1991), 18.

33. Catherine Clifford, "Hedge Fund Billionaire Ray Dalio: Meditation Is 'the Single Most Important Reason' for My Success," *CNBC*, March 16, 2018, https://www.cnbc.com/2018/03/16/bridgewater-associates-ray-dalio-meditation-is-key-to-my-success.html.

34. Tim Ferriss (host), "Yuval Noah Harari on the Story of Sapiens, Forging the Skill of Awareness, and the Power of Disguised Books (#477)," *The Tim Ferris Show* (podcast), https://tim.blog/2020/10/27/yuval-noah-harari/.

35. Daniel Goleman, *Focus: The Hidden Driver of Excellence* (Harper, 2013), 4.

36. Walter Isaacson, *Steve Jobs* (Little, Brown, 2011), 49.

37. James Clear, *Atomic Habits: Tiny Changes, Remarkable Results* (Century, 2018), 72.

38. Mark Williams and Danny Penman, *Mindfulness: A Practical Guide to Finding Peace in a Frantic World* (Piatkus, 2011).

Chapter 5

1. Garry Kasparov, *How Life Imitates Chess: Making the Right Moves, from the Board to the Boardroom* (Bloomsbury, 2008), 4.

2. Paul Rabinow, *Making PCR: A Story of Biotechnology* (University of Chicago Press, 2011), 6–7.

3. Daniel Pink, *A Whole New Mind: Why Right-Brainers Will Rule the Future* (Riverhead, 2006), 1.

4. Pink, *Whole New Mind*, 130.

5. Ed Douglas, "Darwin's Natural Heir," *The Guardian*, February 17, 2001, https://www.theguardian.com/science/2001/feb/17/books.guardianreview57.

6. Edward O. Wilson, *Consilience: The Unity of Knowledge* (Vintage, 1998), 294.

7. Robert G. Hagstrom, *The Essential Buffett: Timeless Principles for the New Economy* (Wiley, 200)1, 20.

8. The concept of mental models was first introduced in Kenneth Craik, *The Nature of Explanation* (Cambridge University Press, 1943) and has since been widely used in cognitive science. It was more recently popularized in the blockbuster by Peter Senge, *The Fifth Discipline: The Art & Practice of the Learning Organization* (Doubleday, 1990).

9. Philosopher Michael Polanyi observed that "we can know more than we can tell" in Michael Polanyi, *The Tacit Dimension* (Doubleday, 1966).

10. Melissa Block, "How the Myers-Briggs Personality Test Began in a Mother's Living Room Lab," *NPR,* September 22, 2018, https://www .npr.org/2018/09/22/650019038/how-the-myers-briggs-personality-test -began-in-a-mothers-living-room-lab.

11. Murray R. Barrick, Michael K. Mount, and Timothy A. Judge, "Personality and Performance at the Beginning of the New Millennium: What Do We Know and Where Do We Go Next?," *International Journal of Selection and Assessment* 9, no. 2 (March 2001), 9–30, https:// doi.org/10.1111/1468-2389.00160.

12. See Amirali Minbashian, Joanne Earl, Jim E.H. Bright," Openness to Experience as a Predictor of Job Performance Trajectories," *Applied Psychology* 62, no. 1, 1–12, https://doi.org/10.1111/j.1464-0597.2012 .00490.x; Christiane Nieß, Hannes Zacher, "Openness to Experience as a Predictor and Outcome of Upward Job Changes into Managerial and Professional Positions," *PLOS One*, 10, no. 6, https://doi.org/10.1371 /journal.pone.0131115; and Hao Zhao, Scott E. Seibert, and G.T. Lumpkin, "The Relationship of Personality to Entrepreneurial Intentions and Performance: A Meta-Analytic Review," *Journal of Management* 36, no. 2, 381–404, https://doi.org/10.1177/0149206309335187.

13. See Yannick Stephan, "Openness to Experience and Active Older Adults' Life Satisfaction: A Trait and Facet-Level Analysis," *Personality and Individual Differences* 47, no. 6 (October 2009), 637–641, https:// doi.org/10.1016/j.paid.2009.05.025; and Paul R. Duberstein, Benjamin P. Chapman, Hilary A. Tindle, Kaycee M. Sink, Patricia Bamonti, John Robbins, Anthony F. Jerant, and Peter Franks, "Personality and Risk for Alzheimer's Disease in Adults 72 Years of Age and Older: A 6-Year Follow-up," *Psychology and Aging* 26, no. 2, 351–362, https:// doi.org/10.1037/a0021377.

14. Scott Barry Kaufman, Colin G. Deyoung, Jeremy R. Gray, Luis Jiménez, Jamie Brown, and Nicholas Mackintosh, "Implicit Learning as an Ability," *Cognition* 116, no. 3 (September 2010), 321–340, https://doi.org/10.1016/j.cognition.2010.05.011.

15. Shane Snow, "A New Way to Become More Open-Minded," *Harvard Business Review*, November 20, 2018, https://hbr.org/2018/11/a-new-way-to-become-more-open-minded.

16. Jesse Martin-Allan, Peter Leeson, and Lesley Sue Martin, "Intentional Personality Change Coaching: A Four-Year Longitudinal Study," *International Coaching Psychology Review* 14, no. 2 (Autumn 2019).

17. T. Schwaba, M. Luhmann, J. J. A. Denissen, J. M. Chung, and W. Bleidorn, "Openness to Experience and Culture-Openness Transactions Across the Lifespan," *Journal of Personality and Social Psychology* 115, no. 1, 118–136, https://doi.org/10.1037/pspp0000150.

18. See for example J. J. Jackson, P. L. Hill, B. R. Payne, B. W. Roberts, and E. A. L. Stine-Morrow, "Can an Old Dog Learn (and Want to Experience) New Tricks? Cognitive Training Increases Openness to Experience in Older Adults," *Psychology and Aging* 27, no. 2, 286–292, https://doi.org/10.1037/a0025918.

19. Mark T. Wagner, Michael C. Mithoefer, Ann T. Mithoefer, Rebecca K. MacAulay, Lisa Jerome, Berra Yazar-Klosinski, and Rick Doblin, "Therapeutic Effect of Increased Openness: Investigating Mechanism of Action in MDMA-Assisted Psychotherapy," *Journal of Psychopharmacology* 31, no. 8 (August 1, 2017), 967–974, https://doi.org/10.1177/0269881117711712; and Katherine A. MacLean, Matthew W. Johnson, and Roland R. Griffiths, "Mystical Experiences Occasioned by the Hallucinogen Psilocybin Lead to Increases in the Personality Domain of Openness," *Journal of Psychopharmacology* 25, no. 11 (November 1, 2011), 1453–1461, https://doi.org/10.1177/0269881111420188.

20. Erica Fink, "When Silicon Valley Takes LSD," *CNN Business*, January 25, 2015, https://money.cnn.com/2015/01/25/technology/lsd-psychedelics-silicon-valley/.

21. Keith Johnstone, *Impro: Improvisation and the Theatre* (Eyre Methuen, 1981), 25.

22. Johnstone, *Impro*, 130.

23. Farhad Manjoo, "Dick Costolo Thinks It's O.K. to Never Tweet," *New York Times*, February 25, 2015, https://www.nytimes.com/2015/03/01/magazine/dick-costolo-thinks-its-ok-to-never-tweet.html.

24. Rosabeth Moss Kanter, "Strategy as Improvisational Theater," *MIT Sloan Management Review*, Winter 2002, January 15, 2002, https://sloanreview.mit.edu/article/strategy-as-improvisational-theater/.

25. Jens Förster, Ronald S. Friedman, Eva B. Butterbach, and Kai Sassenberg, "Automatic Effects of Deviancy Cues on Creative Cognition," *European Journal of Social Psychology* 35, no. 3 (May/June 2005), 345–359, https://doi.org/10.1002/ejsp.253.

26. Yaacov Trope and Nira Liberman, "Construal-Level Theory of Psychological Distance," *Psychological Review* 117, no. 2 (April 2010), 440–463, https://doi.org/10.1037/a0018963.

27. Karen W. Pryor, Richard Haag, and Joseph O'Reilly, "The Creative Porpoise: Training for Novel Behavior," *Journal of the Experimental Analysis of Behavior* 12, no. 4 (July 1969), 653–661, https://doi.org/10.1901/jeab.1969.12-653.

28. Allen Neuringer, "Reinforced Variability in Animals and People: Implications for Adaptive Action," *American Psychologist* 59, no. 9 (2004), 891–906, https://doi.org/10.1037/0003-066X.59.9.891.

29. F. Scott Fitzgerald, "The Crack-up," *Esquire*, February 1936.

30. Lewis Carroll, *Through the Looking-Glass, and What Alice Found There* (Macmillan, 1871), 69.

31. Ella Miron-Spektor, Francesca Gino, and Linda Argote, "Paradoxical Frames and Creative Sparks: Enhancing Individual Creativity Through Conflict and Integration," *Organizational Behavior and Human Decision Processes* 116, no. 2 (2011), 229–240, https://doi.org/10.1016/j.obhdp.2011.03.006.

32. Ella Miron-Spektor, Amy Ingram, Joshua Keller, Wendy K. Smith, and Marianne W. Lewis, "Microfoundations of Organizational Paradox: The Problem Is How We Think about the Problem," *Academy of Management Journal* 61, no. 1 (March 16, 2017), https://doi.org/10.5465/amj.2016.0594.

33. Devi Shetty, "How Mother Teresa Touched My Heart Writes Dr Devi Shetty," *DNA*, December 4, 2016, https://www.dnaindia.com/india/comment-how-mother-teresa-touched-my-heart-1428877.

34. Ari Alstedter, "The World's Cheapest Hospital Has to Get Even Cheaper," *Bloomberg Businessweek*, March 26, 2019, https://www.bloomberg.com/news/features/2019-03-26/the-world-s-cheapest-hospital-has-to-get-even-cheaper.

35. Albert Rothenberg, "Janusian Thinking and Nobel Prize Laureates," *American Journal of Psychiatry*, February 1982, https://10.1176/ajp.139.1.122.

36. First part of the quote from George E. P. Box, "Science and Statistics," *Journal of the American Statistical Association* 71, no. 356, 791–799, doi: 10.1080/01621459.1976.10480949, second part from George E. P. Box, "Some Problems of Statistics and Everyday Life," *Journal of the American Statistical Association* 74, no. (365), 1–4, doi:10.2307/2286713.

37. Apparently never said by Keynes though he frequently expressed similar sentiments. See "When the Facts Change, I Change My Mind. What Do You Do, Sir?" *Quote Investigator*, July 22, 2011, https:// quoteinvestigator.com/2011/07/22/keynes-change-mind/.

38. Thomas S. Kuhn, *The Structure of Scientific Revolutions* (University of Chicago Press, 1962).

39. Reported in Jason Fried, "Some Advice from Jeff Bezos," *Signal v Noise*, August 27, 2018, https://m.signalvnoise.com/some-advice-from-jeff -bezos/.

40. "Jeff Bezos Shares His Management Style and Philosophy," Geekwire channel, YouTube, 3:32, https://www.youtube.com/watch?v=F7JMMy -yHSU.

41. Paul Graham, "Keep Your Identity Small," *Paul Graham* (blog), http:// www.paulgraham.com/identity.html.

42. Shane Parrish (host), "Ben Thompson: Thriving in a Digital World," *The Knowledge Project* (podcast), Episode 40, https://fs.blog/knowledge -podcast/ben-thompson/.

43. Kat Eschner, "The Farmboy Who Invented Television," *Smithsonian Magazine*, August 28, 2017, https://www.smithsonianmag.com/smart -news/farmboy-who-invented-television-while-plowing-180964607/.

44. Kounios and Beeman, *The Eureka Factor*, 65–71, 84–85.

45. See https://academic.oup.com/cercor/article/17/2/314/316404?login =true and https://www.sciencedirect.com/science/article/abs/pii/S0361 923011002280.

46. Kounios and Beeman, *The Eureka Factor*, 84.

47. Kounios and Beeman, *The Eureka Factor*, 87.

48. Andrew W. Bailey and Eric Hungenberg, "Psychogeography of a Marathon Runner: An Exploratory EEG Approach," *Journal of Sport Behavior* 42, no. 4 (December 2019), 415–440.

49. Douglas P. Lackey, "What Are the Modern Classics? The Baruch Poll of Great Philosophy in the Twentieth Century," *The Philosophical Forum* XXX, no. 4 (December 1999), https://www.stephanwetzels.nl /wordpress/docs/Lackey-What-are-the-modern-classics.pdf.

50. Ross Dawson (host), "Cathy Hackl on Finding the Key Players to Listen to, Building Mental Maps, How to See Connections, and

Becoming a Voice in Your Industry (Ep2)," *Thriving on Overload* (podcast), December 14, 2021, https://thrivingonoverload.com/cathy -hackl-finding-key-players-building-mental-maps-see-connection/.

51. Bret Stetka, "Spark Creativity with Thomas Edison's Napping Technique," *Scientific American*, December 9, 2021, https://www .scientificamerican.com/article/thomas-edisons-naps-inspire-a-way-to -spark-your-own-creativity/.

52. Colleen M. Seifert, David E. Meyer, Natalie Davidson, Andrea L. Patalano, and Ilan Yaniv. "Demystification of cognitive insight: Opportunistic assimilation and the prepared-mind hypothesis." In R. Sternberg, & J. Davidson (Eds.), *The Nature of Insight* (MIT Press, 1994), 65–124.

53. M. K. Wisehart, "Making Your Imagination Work for You," *The American Magazine*, April 1921, https://teslauniverse.com/nikola-tesla/articles /making-your-imagination-work-you.

54. Kounios and Beeman, *The Eureka Factor*, 212–213.

55. Robert Coram, "John Boyd—USAF: The Fighter Pilot Who Changed the Art of Air Warfare," *Aviation History*, http://www.aviation-history .com/airmen/boyd.htm.

56. Eric Ries, "Principles of Lean Startups, Presentation for Maples Investments," *Startup Lessons Learned*, November 4, 2008, http://www .startuplessonslearned.com/2008/11/principles-of-lean-startups.html.

57. Annie Duke, *Thinking in Bets: Making Smarter Decisions When You Don't Have All the Facts* (Portfolio, 2018), 2.

58. Duke, *Thinking in Bets*, 26.

59. Duke, *Thinking in Bets*, 112.

60. The concept was originally proposed in Charles G. Lord, Mark R. Lepper, and Elizabeth Preston, "Considering the Opposite: A Corrective Strategy for Social Judgment," *Journal of Personality and Social Psychology* 47, no. 6 (1984), 1231, https://doi.org/10.1037/0022-3514.47.6.1231; Larrick's question was first shared in R. P. Larrick, "Debiasing," in D. J. Koehler and N. Harvey (eds.), *Blackwell Handbook of Judgment and Decision Making* (Blackwell Publishing, 2007), 323, https://psycnet.apa.org/record/2004 -19929-016 and https://psycnet.apa.org/buy/1992-04093-001.

61. Brendan Mulvaney, "Red Team: Strengthening Through Challenge," *Marine Corps Gazette*, July 2012, 63–66, https://www.hqmc.marines .mil/Portals/138/Docs/PL/PLU/Mulvaney.pdf.

62. Tim Ferriss (host), "Marc Andreessen—Lessons, Predictions, and Recommendations from an Icon (#163)," *The Tim Ferriss Show* (podcast), March 29, 2016, https://tim.blog/2016/05/29/marc-andreessen/.

63. Matt Bodnar (host), "Blindspots, Bias, Billionaires and Bridgewater with Dr. Adam Grant," *The Success Podcast*, March 29, 2018, https://www.successpodcast.com/show-notes/2018/3/28/blindspots-bias-billionaires-and-bridgewater-with-dr-adam-grant.
64. Reed Hastings, "Reed Hastings on Netflix's Biggest Mistake," *Forbes*, September 11, 2020, https://www.forbes.com/sites/forbesdigitalcovers/2020/09/11/reed-hastings-no-rules-rules-book-excerpt-netflix-biggest-mistake/.

Chapter 6

1. "Announcing the 2016 Fuller Challenge Finalists," Buckminster Fuller Institute, https://www.bfi.org/2016/08/19/announcing-the-2016-fuller-challenge-finalists/.
2. Elinor Mills, "Google's Excellent Adventure," *CNN*, June 28, 2005, https://www.cnet.com/news/googles-excellent-adventure/.
3. David Perell, "The Paradox of Abundance," https://perell.com/note/the-paradox-of-abundance/.
4. Susan Greenfield, *Mind Change: How Digital Technologies Are Leaving Their Mark on Our Brains* (Random House, 2015), xiii.
5. Greenfield, *Mind Change*.
6. Martin Robbins, "Mind Change: Susan Greenfield Has a Big Idea, but What Is It?," *The Guardian*, October 3, 2014, https://www.theguardian.com/science/the-lay-scientist/2014/oct/03/mind-change-susan-greenfield-has-a-big-idea-but-what-is-it.
7. Aimee J. Ellington, "The Effects of Non-CAS Graphing Calculators on Student Achievement and Attitude Levels in Mathematics: A Meta-Analysis," *School Science and Mathematics* 106, no. 1 (January 2006), 16–26, https://doi.org/10.1111/j.1949-8594.2006.tb18067.x.
8. Bob Weinhold, "Epigenetics: The Science of Change," *Environmental Health Perspectives* 114, no. 3 (2006), A160–7, https://doi.org/10.1289/ehp.114-a160.
9. Martin I. Lind and Foteini Spagopoulou, "Evolutionary Consequences of Epigenetic Inheritance," *Heredity* 121 (2018), 205–209, https://doi.org/10.1038/s41437-018-0113-y.
10. Ramez Naam, *The Infinite Resource: The Power of Ideas on a Finite Planet* (University Press of New England, 2013).
11. Russ Juskalian, "Interview with Clay Shirky, Part I," *Columbia Journalism Review*, December 19, 2008, https://archives.cjr.org/overload/interview_with_clay_shirky_par.php.

INDEX

Page numbers followed by *f* refer to figures.

ABOUT THE AUTHOR

Ross Dawson believes the future is ours to create. He is globally recognized as a leading futurist, keynote speaker, entrepreneur, and authority on business strategy. Ross is founding chairman of the Advanced Human Technologies group of companies, and the bestselling author of four previous books including the acclaimed *Living Networks*. Strong global demand has seen him deliver keynote speeches and strategy workshops to business and government leaders in over 30 countries, with clients including the likes of Boston Consulting Group, Citibank, Coca-Cola, EY, Google, Interpublic Group, News Limited, Oracle, Procter & Gamble, PwC, Roche, Visa, and Walmart. He appears frequently in media such as ABC TV, BBC, *Die Welt*, *El País*, the *Guardian*, *Le Monde*, the *New York Times*, *Sunrise*, *Today*, *VICE*, and many others.

For more information, visit rossdawson.com.